Former corporate lawyer, co-founder of a successful software company and technology investor David Gillespie is the bestselling author of the *Sweet Poison* books, *Big Fat Lies*, *Free Schools*, *Eat Real Food*, *The Eat Real Food Cookbook*, *Taming Toxic People* and *Teen Brain*. He lives in Brisbane with his wife and six children.

THE GOOD FAT GUIDE

David Gillespie

MACMILLAN
Pan Macmillan Australia

First published 2019 in Macmillan by Pan Macmillan Australia Pty Ltd
1 Market Street, Sydney, New South Wales, Australia, 2000

Cataloguing-in-Publication entry is available
from the National Library of Australia
http://catalogue.nla.gov.au

Typeset in 11/18pt Sabon LT by Midland Typesetters, Australia
Printed by McPherson's Printing Group
Illustrations by Kirby Armstrong

The paper in this book is FSC® certified.
FSC® promotes environmentally responsible,
socially beneficial and economically viable
management of the world's forests.

For Lizzie, Anthony, James, Gwen, Adam, Elisabeth and Fin

Contents

Introduction

Vegetable oil makes you exceedingly vulnerable to cancer. Every mouthful of vegetable oil you consume takes you one step closer to a deadly and irreversible outcome. Every mouthful of vegetable oil you feed to your family is doing the same to them. You are eating 'vegetable oil' because it is much cheaper to chemically extract oils from plant seeds than it is to raise and slaughter an animal or grow a coconut tree. And you are being told to eat it for your health by nutrition advocates who have been successfully and thoroughly hoodwinked by the food industry.

I am telling you this not because I am a conspiracy theorist or a herbal-gerbil knit-your-own-food purveyor. I am telling you because if you knew this (and could prove it) and didn't tell me and my family, I'd be furious with you. I am not a doctor or a nutritionist. I have no formal training in human biochemistry or even chemistry. I am a lawyer and the only relevant skill I bring to the table is an ability to gather, understand and synthesise evidence. Science is based on people making hypotheses about how things might work and then collecting evidence that will prove them right (or wrong). Just like law, science should be all about the evidence. However, when it comes to the river of gold flowing to the processed food industry, evidence runs smack bang into commercial interest and, unfortunately for us, commercial interest generally wins out.

Two hundred years ago, humans ate approximately what they had been eating for 10,000 (or, in some cases, 200,000) years prior. Where they lived and how much money they had affected the exact mix, but in general the diet was a mixture of vegetables, legumes and nuts, grains, meat, fish and occasional fruit. Fish didn't have fingers and chickens hadn't learnt how to grow nuggets. The only fat you were likely to encounter was in a piece of meat or, if you lived near the equator, in tropical fruits such as avocados and coconuts. Sugar was even rarer and could usually only be obtained after a protracted series of negotiations with stinging insects. If you think you still eat like that, have a quick check of your pantry or fridge. If all you find are cuts of whole meat, whole fruit and vegetables, wholegrains or flours, eggs and milk, then you don't need this book. Put it down and continue to lead a healthy (and probably long) life. If instead you find lots of boxes, tins and bottles with pictures of food on them rather than actual food, then you need to read further.

You're still here? Well, let's get down to the purpose of this book. In my first book, *Sweet Poison*, I looked at what science says about the sugar that has been added to our food in escalating quantities since the advent of commercial sugar production in the early

1800s. I documented the scientific evidence, now well-established, which proves convincingly that the fructose half of sugar is a lethal addition to our diet. I also talked briefly about the measures my family had undertaken to find and remove it from our diet. In *Big Fat Lies*, I started to examine the evidence on dietary fat. I had seen this evidence from the corner of my eye as I was reading about fructose. I knew that fat was not a dietary bogeyman once appetite control was restored (by removing fructose), but I had noticed that something like the sugar story had been happening in the world of fat.

WHAT IS A VEGETABLE OIL?

Well, it ain't oil from vegetables. Vegetable oil is edible fat extracted from plants rather than animals. It includes oils from fruit (such as avocado, olives and coconuts), oils from nuts (such as macadamias), oils from legumes (such as peanuts and soybeans), and oils from seeds (such as almonds, cottonseeds, grapeseed, sunflowers, rice bran and canola).

As a rule, the oils from legumes and seeds are the cheapest of these and the most widely used. They're also deadly because they tend to be high in polyunsaturated fat and, more particularly, omega-6 fat. You'll find out why this matters below.

The story of fat

Between 1820 and 1920, the world's population doubled from 1 billion to 2 billion. Nothing like this had ever happened before.

It took us a quarter of a million years to get to the first billion but the second billion came in just a century. Not surprisingly, our ability to feed everybody was being stretched to breaking point and prices of food – particularly animal-based products – began to spiral upward. This provided an incentive to come up with food-like products made from cheaper raw materials.

Humans are endlessly ingenious and when that ingenuity was applied to the problem of expensive animal fat and animal-fat products like butter, a solution was quickly discovered. It turned out that if enough pressure and heat was applied, fats could be extracted from things that were otherwise going to waste, such as cottonseeds. Treated with the right chemicals, these fats could be made to look and behave just like the animal fats we had consumed for millennia. Just like sugar, these new, cheap fats made their way into our food supply. At first they were cooking fats and margarines, and then shortenings used in baked goods, but eventually they found their way into almost every food on the supermarket shelf, because there are very few foods that don't taste better with a little fat.

In commerce, it is rare to do the cheapest thing and be seen to do the right thing. Dumping industrial waste into rivers is cheaper than disposing of it properly, but no one will applaud you for doing it. Using second-hand car parts is cheaper than using new ones but few people will thank you for it if you charge them for new. However, when it comes to edible oils, doing things the cheap way gets you a round of applause from the guardians of our nutritional health. Indeed, the Australian Heart Foundation and the Dietitians Association of Australia, to name two such groups, actively encourage us to consume products that use seed oils instead of animal fats, such as margarine in preference to butter.

Their encouragement is based on evidence that could be described as flimsy at best, and there is significant evidence which says exactly the opposite, but it does not force them to alter their industry-sponsored position.

In *Big Fat Lies*, I looked in detail at the insidious danger that lies in those man-made fats. Fructose is dangerous because our bodies are not genetically adapted to a diet that contains it in industrial quantities. The same can be said for the polyunsaturated fats which dominate the oils extracted from seeds. Our extraordinarily complex biochemistry works on the assumption that we will have a very small quantity of these fats in our diet and that every other fat we consume will come from animals or other sources of saturated or monounsaturated fat (see page 12 for an explanation of the different types of fat). That was a reasonable assumption before around 1850, but the recent replacement of almost all fats with their cheaper cousins has meant that it is now almost impossible to buy food that is not full of seed oil.

It is now almost impossible to buy food that is not full of seed oil.

In Chapter 1 of this book, I review the history of how we got to this point and look closely at the evidence about seed oils. If you've read *Big Fat Lies*, much of this will be familiar to you, although I have included more recent reviews of the evidence where available. I've also looked further into the damage that an excess of seed oils, in particular omega-6 seed oils, can cause to our eyes, our reproductive abilities and our immune systems and, critically, how they increase our and our children's risk of suffering from cancer. If you don't like science and are happy to accept that seed oils should be avoided, feel free to skip to Chapter 2.

For the past decade, I've tried to avoid seed oils. Chapter 2 describes the results of my endeavours. It is easy to say that our food supply looks nothing like it did 200 years ago, but it's simply not possible for 7 billion of us (and counting) to live and eat the way 1 billion of us did then. If you want to eat whole food and nothing else, you're already avoiding both added fructose and added seed oils. But if, like me, you have neither the time nor the inclination to assemble everything you eat from scratch, then you need the research set out here. I go through each of the major categories of prepared food, looking for the seed oils hidden within, and suggest which choices are best. In doing so, I am also keeping an eye on the fructose content. For most food categories, I provide you with a brand recommendation which contains the least possible fructose and the least possible seed oil. Sometimes, however, there is simply no viable choice, and that's when you'll need Chapter 3.

In Chapter 3, I set out recipes developed by my wife, Lizzie. We use most of these recipes – many of them on a weekly or even daily basis – to replace foods that cannot be easily purchased without seed oil or sugar. You won't find too many desserts in this section. (If that's what you want, you need the recipes in my books *The Eat Real Food Cookbook* and *The Sweet Poison Quit Plan Cookbook*.) These recipes are for the savoury essentials – like fried food, mayo, pestos and spreads – and you will probably want them if you plan to live without seed oil.

This is not a weight-loss book, but it is a diet book. If you eat the way I suggest, you will lose weight if you need to because, besides cutting out seed oils, you will also avoid added sugar. Your appetite control will function the way it should, and you will stop eating when you have sufficient energy. It's that simple. You won't find me encouraging you to purchase purple pears grown on the south side of the hill and picked at midnight on a Tuesday, or suggesting you supplement your food with potions and powders to enhance their nutritional value, or telling you to count calories or exercise more. I will simply be telling you what not to buy if you want to live longer than you otherwise might, and look good while you're doing it.

Sugar has given us diabetes, dementia and obesity. Polyunsaturated fats have given us cancer, multiple sclerosis and other autoimmune diseases as well as destroying fertility. In just three generations, they've combined to give us heart disease and to create other seemingly untreatable chronic disease epidemics. Both were added to our diets in bulk long before any ingredients were tested for their health impacts or safety. Just 200 years ago, barely any of these diseases existed at a significant level. But now they consume almost all the Western world's healthcare budgets, and the costs continue to grow more quickly than any nation can support. These diseases have raced from obscurity to epidemic proportions during a period when our health authorities have told us to replace animal fats with seed oil and have ignored sugar altogether. To this day those 'experts' warn us against consuming animal fats, but it's difficult not to comply because animal fat is jolly hard to get. It's all gone. Barely a manufactured food now exists which has not had any skerrick of animal fat replaced with seed oils. My purpose in this book is to ensure that you are not another victim of the industrialisation of your food supply. I want to provide you with a seed-oil and sugar avoidance sat-nav for your local supermarket. If you do what I suggest, you'll be eating butter, drinking full-fat milk, chomping through bacon and eggs for breakfast and enjoying a meat pie for lunch. According to our health authorities, you will be doing all the wrong things, but the science says you will significantly increase your chances of living a longer and hopefully happy life. Bon appétit!

1

Big fat lies

Today's standard nutrition advice is that we should eat less animal fat, and most of us have taken this advice with gusto. It's why the supermarkets can get away with selling lean meat for twice the price of meat with the fat still attached, and why a 'healthy' margarine, stuffed to the brim with polyunsaturated vegetable oil, can be three or four times the price of ordinary butter.

The 'eat less fat' message is dispensed by almost everyone who feels they can tell us what to eat, driving much of the front-of-pack 'healthy eating' labelling we see every day – 'light', 'low-fat' and '99% fat-free' – winking at us from every shelf.

The Australian Government's Australian Guide to Healthy Eating is the gold-standard for nutrition advice in this country. Dare to question the standard message and you'll eventually be directed back to this guide. They tell

> **The 'eat less fat' message is dispensed by almost everyone who feels they can tell us what to eat.**

us to: 'Replace high fat foods which contain predominantly saturated fats such as butter, cream, cooking margarine, coconut and palm oil with foods which contain predominantly polyunsaturated and monounsaturated fats such as oils, spreads, nut butters/pastes and avocado.' The reason is pretty obvious, according to the writers: eating fat makes us overweight. And because being overweight is a risk factor for type 2 diabetes, eating fat is believed to cause that as well.

According to the guide, dietary fat also causes coronary heart disease, but by a more convoluted route. Apparently, some of the fat we eat causes our cholesterol to rise, and since high cholesterol is a risk factor for heart disease, we should stop eating fat if we want to avoid that.

The only trouble with all of this is that it's just plain wrong. The evidence doesn't support any of these claims, and it's becoming increasingly clear that the things we use to replace dietary animal fat – usually sugar and seed oils – are likely to be the real cause not just of heart disease, but also of type 2 diabetes, cancers and obesity.

THE MINNESOTA CORONARY EXPERIMENT (MCE)

In 1968, the US government funded the largest ever trial aimed at proving that saturated fat caused heart disease. The MCE was conducted from 1968 to 1973 and involved almost 10,000 individuals in a double-blind, randomised controlled trial of a dietary intervention. The trial tested just one thing: the effect of replacing saturated fat with omega-6 fat.

The intervention diet reduced dietary fat from 18.5 per cent to 9.2 per cent of calories and increased omega-6 fats from 3.4 per cent to 13.2 per cent. This was achieved by replacing cooking fats and salad dressings with corn oil, trimming meat, switching to low-fat dairy and swapping from butter to margarine.

Despite the massive investment of money and time, the results of the study never saw the light of day. There was just one journal paper, published in 1989, which concluded that replacing the fats didn't lower the risk of heart disease or death.

In 2016, investigators from the US National Institutes of Health were able to access the original data and publish the results. They were not good for the traditional story on saturated fat and heart disease.

The results showed that switching to seed oil did indeed lower blood cholesterol, by an average of 14 per cent, but that did not help people live longer. The lower the cholesterol fell, the greater the risk of dying. People were 22 per cent more likely to die for every 30 mg/dL (0.78 mmol/L) reduction in blood cholesterol. The authors argued that the likely reason for this increase was that while the seed oils clearly reduced the number of LDL cholesterol particles, they made them more susceptible to oxidation. Oxidised LDL is now generally considered a major heart disease risk factor.

The results backed up a similar reanalysis of the Sydney Diet Heart Study, another rigorously conducted trial commenced in 1966. That reanalysis also found that the replacement of saturated fat with seed oils increased the likelihood of death from any cause by 62 per cent and from heart disease by 70 per cent.

How polyunsaturated fats harm us

The fats that dominate in vegetable oils are highly unstable. When they interact with heat and oxygen, they release neuro-toxic, DNA-mutating chemicals which are known to cause cancer, at least. Recent improvements in technology have now thrown a spotlight on the quantity of these chemicals released by normal use in cooking, and the results are truly terrifying.

Vegetable oil made from seeds (canola, sunflower, corn, safflower, grapeseed, rice bran and soybean oils, for example) is a relatively new addition to the human diet. Unlike animal fats and oils made from fruit (olive, avocado and coconut oils), they're very high in polyunsaturated fats and in particular omega-6 fat.

When we eat polyunsaturated fats, they become embedded in our cell membranes, where they are prone to attack by oxygen molecules. We can handle that when our polyunsaturated-fat intake is at the level it has been traditionally in our food supply because we have evolved defences against the damage they can cause.

The two primary polyunsaturated fats in our diet are omega-3 and omega-6. Unless we take supplements, we are unlikely to overconsume omega-3, but seed-based vegetable oils are very high in omega-6. When we overconsume any polyunsaturated fat, we overwhelm our antioxidant defences and an out-of-control chain reaction known as oxidative stress occurs. This chain reaction results in the production of some highly toxic chemicals, including MDA (malondialdehyde) and 4-HNE (4-hydroxynonenal). They're

When we overconsume any polyunsaturated fat, we overwhelm our antioxidant defences and an out-of-control chain reaction known as oxidative stress occurs.

dangerous because they interact destructively with our DNA and significantly increase the chances that cancer will develop. But that's by no means the worst of it. Because of their neurotoxic capabilities, these molecules and others like them are likely to be heavily involved in Alzheimer's disease, motor neurone disease, multiple sclerosis and Parkinson's disease. They're also implicated in chronic inflammation, the recent massive increase in allergies, stroke and heart disease and, less predictably, they probably lie behind the sudden mass decline in male fertility and increase in childhood cancer.

THERE WAS AN OLD LADY WHO SWALLOWED A FLY . . .

This nursery rhyme from the mid-20th century tells the story of an old woman who swallows a fly. She then swallows a spider to catch the fly. Then she swallows a bird to catch the spider. It continues with her swallowing increasingly larger animals to get rid of the one she's just swallowed until, eventually, she swallows a horse and dies.

The story of vegetable oils is similar. We initially used vegetable oils because they were cheap, but they didn't work as well as the more solid saturated fats, so we turned them into trans fats (man-made equivalents of saturated fats). Then we discovered trans fats were bad for us so we started using palm oil because it could still be labelled as 'vegetable oil' but had much higher levels of saturated fat. And then the orangutans got wiped out because palm oil farming destroys their habitat.

Similarly, because vegetable oils are so unstable and prone to oxidation, we add antioxidant chemicals so they don't decay in foods. Unfortunately, we've just discovered that one of the most popular antioxidants used in these oils significantly decreases the effectiveness of the flu vaccine.

No one wants to become the old lady who swallowed the fly – and the best way to do that is to avoid consuming vegetable oils in the first place.

Eleven ways polyunsaturated fat will hurt you

This is a fast-moving area of scientific research and new potential consequences of polyunsaturated fat overconsumption are being proposed and tested very rapidly. This list is just a taste of eleven risks you take when consuming seed oils.

1. Polyunsaturated fats cause cancer

Our cells normally die and replicate according to a schedule. They have DNA switches that tell them when they should replicate and when to die. If those DNA switches are damaged by oxidation caused by polyunsaturated fats, the damaged cells can become a breeding ground for potential cancer growth. We can compensate for DNA damage and most of it does no permanent harm at all, but every now and then, DNA damage produces a mutation that would help the next generation of cells become cancerous.

The risk of cancer has always been and always will be with us. It's a consequence of having cells that replicate imperfectly. However, omega-6 consumption at least doubles our chances of developing cancer. Even worse, it appears that in some cases that omega-6 fats act to disable the natural genetic defences that are supposed to protect us against cancer. And if that weren't bad enough, it is likely that fats you consume now could be responsible for cancers in your children.

2. Polyunsaturated fats cause childhood cancers

Childhood cancers are defined as those diagnosed before the child turns fourteen. Together, leukaemia (blood cell cancers), brain tumours and lymphomas account for more than two-thirds of all childhood cancers, but leukaemia is by far the most common.

Omega-6 consumption at least doubles our chances of developing cancer. Even worse, it appears that in some cases that omega-6 fats act to disable the natural genetic defences that are supposed to protect us against cancer.

One in 500 Australian children will develop cancer. That's two new cases every day, one of the highest rates in the world, and it is getting much worse very quickly. A child born in the UK in 1911 was six times less likely to suffer from leukaemia than one born today. Australian statistics show identical trends.

The genetic damage that lies behind most childhood cancer is caused by oxidative damage to sperm DNA. Oxidative stress produces highly toxic and reactive end products which attack the integrity of the DNA carried by sperm. We normally deal with heavily disrupted cell DNA by repairing it or killing off the damaged cell. Unfortunately, this is not always the case with sperm. Human sperm sometimes retain the capacity for fertilisation even when their DNA are severely damaged (and this is even more likely with modern assisted reproduction techniques).

We know this for certain because of studies done in men who smoke. Even though those studies have shown smokers are much less fertile than non-smokers, they are not always infertile. The sperm of smokers who remain fertile have DNA that has been damaged by oxidative stress caused by the inhalation of aldehydes which promote oxidation.

Because sperm with damaged DNA are still able to create viable embryos, the consequences can be cataclysmic. We have known since at least 1997 that the children of fathers who smoke heavily are four to five times as likely to develop childhood cancers.

Intentionally inhaling toxic aldehydes by smoking is therefore obviously a bad idea for men thinking about having children. But in the last 50 years, Australia's male smoking rates have been diving almost as fast as the rates of childhood cancer have been increasing. Now less than one in five men smoke (down from three in four after the Second World War) and more than half have never smoked.

Smoking is clearly not the only source of toxic aldehydes in our environment. We also manufacture them ourselves if we consume too much omega-6 polyunsaturated fat and we can be significantly exposed to them if we inhale the vapours from heating those fats (see more on this on page 22).

It is no surprise then that as oxidation fuel increases in the form of vegetable oil in our food, so too will the rate of childhood cancers. If we do nothing about the presence of these fats in our food, we can expect to see the rate of those cancers continue to climb dramatically.

3. Polyunsaturated fats help fructose cause heart disease

The research now clearly shows that the oxidation of small dense LDL cholesterol (the 'bad cholesterol' particles exported by our liver when we eat fructose) is the primary cause of heart disease. The very best way to have that sort of particle in your bloodstream is to eat sugar, and the very best way to ensure it is oxidised is to eat omega-6 fats.

4. Polyunsaturated fats make you blind

Macular degeneration is the primary cause of blindness in Australia today. One in seven Australians over the age of 50 (a little over a million people) has the disease, and this number is likely to increase by at least 70 per cent by 2030. Macular degeneration is caused by waste accumulating in our eyes, which happens if there's more omega-6 than omega-3 polyunsaturated fat in our diet.

Macular degeneration is caused by waste accumulating in our eyes, which happens if there's more omega-6 than omega-3 polyunsaturated fat in our diet.

Use of seed oils significantly increases both the amount of omega-6 and the ratio of omega-6 to omega-3. This isn't controversial science, but you won't find macular degeneration researchers or charities telling you about it. This is probably because to do so would be to directly contradict the advice of the Heart Foundation.

5. Polyunsaturated fats cause Parkinson's disease

The 4-HNE produced from omega-6 fats, either by the process of oxidative stress, or directly ingested or inhaled from cooking, is a neurotoxin that's particularly destructive to the neurons that control our ability to move. When those neurons are damaged, they're not replaced. If we lose enough of them, we have Parkinson's disease, a progressive loss of motor control of our body.

Because the disease is the result of cumulative destruction, it's most prevalent in people over 50, but 20 per cent of cases are now diagnosed between 20 and 50. Michael J. Fox was diagnosed when he was just 30. There are very few places in the world where accurate long-term statistics have been kept on the incidence of Parkinson's disease, but they've done just that in Olmsted County, Minnesota (population 147,066). Researchers there have concluded that annual new cases almost doubled between 1944 and 1984 (using consistent diagnostic rules). That is not to say this is irrefutable proof of a relationship between Parkinson's and polyunsaturated fat, but it certainly lends credence to the likelihood of one.

6. Polyunsaturated fats give you rheumatoid arthritis

Every day, seventeen Australians have a joint replaced because of rheumatoid arthritis, and the number of us with the disease is accelerating quickly. Hospitalisation for rheumatoid arthritis (largely for joint replacement) has been steadily increasing and doubled in the first decade of the 21st century alone. Alarmingly, it appears that the incidence is increasing even more rapidly in children, for whom the rate of hospitalisation more than tripled over the same time frame.

Rheumatoid arthritis is an autoimmune disease – a disease caused by our immune system attacking bits of us. Omega-6 fats drive the inflammation response of our immune system.

Rheumatoid arthritis is an autoimmune disease – a disease caused by our immune system attacking bits of us. Omega-6 fats drive the inflammation response of our immune system, and we know for certain that if we reduce the amount of omega-6 in the diet, rheumatoid arthritis symptoms improve. The standard advice for rheumatoid arthritis is to increase the amount of omega-3 in an attempt to redress the balance, but that will also increase the total polyunsaturated fat in the system and this is not a good thing. It's better to just stop consuming the seed oils that contain omega-6 in the first place.

7. Polyunsaturated fats give you multiple sclerosis

As debilitating as rheumatoid arthritis is, it's just one of a series of diseases on the same autoimmune spectrum. Like rheumatoid arthritis, multiple sclerosis (MS) is caused by the immune system attacking part of the body, namely myelin, the fatty sheath that serves as the electrical insulation for the brain, spinal cord and nerves. Over time, the accumulated damage results in our neurons losing function and no longer being able to communicate.

We know that the immediate cause of an autoimmune attack is a failure of that part of our immune system responsible for shutting down our immune response. We also know that two things in particular will degrade the function of that part of the immune system: omega-6 fat consumption and a fatty liver, caused by sugar overconsumption.

The process of coating our brain and spinal cord in myelin is incomplete when we're born. In fact, it's barely started. It takes us about 25 years to get the job fully done. We know that omega-6 fats deactivate the cells that produce the myelin. If during those first 25 years we're exposed to significant quantities of omega-6 fats, we may be laying the groundwork for autoimmune attacks later in life. That's speculation at the moment, but when it comes to my kids, I don't take the risk.

8. Polyunsaturated fats give you osteoporosis

One in 20 Australians has osteoporosis (Greek for 'porous bones'), one in four has low-bone density (the precursor to osteoporosis) and the number of people affected is accelerating. In the last ten years, the number of GP visits in Australia related to osteoporosis has doubled. We know that the polyunsaturated omega-3s that predominate some fish oils, flaxseeds and kelp help us build up bone density, while the omega-6 oils that predominate in seed oils destroy it.

9. Polyunsaturated fats cause allergies and asthma

One in four Australians now suffers from an allergic or immune disease, and the numbers are increasing at obscene rates. Reported rates of hay fever, asthma and eczema have doubled in the last fifteen years. Hospitalisation rates for the most extreme form of allergic reaction, anaphylaxis (life-threatening acute inflammation, usually in response to food), also doubled between 1994 and 2005. The biggest overall change has been a five-fold increase in hospital admissions for children up to the age of four as compared to just double for the rest of the population. That's a five-fold increase in just ten years! It's not your imagination or the explosion in helicopter parenting, there actually is a lot more allergic disease around today.

What all these diseases have in common is that they're part of our immune system's inflammatory response. Studies have shown that children who consume more margarine,

Studies have shown that children who consume more margarine, which is made from seed oils, have double the rate of medically diagnosed eczema, hay fever, allergies and asthma.

which is made from seed oils, have double the rate of medically diagnosed eczema, hay fever, allergies and asthma. Even when the kids themselves aren't chomping on margarine or vegetable oils, if their mother did during the last four weeks of pregnancy, they have at least a 50 per cent greater chance of having eczema, hay fever or allergies for life.

10. Polyunsaturated fats reduce cognitive ability

Sizeable chunks of the human brain are made from polyunsaturated fats and their derivatives. Our cognitive ability is directly linked to the amount of and ratio of each of the polyunsaturated fats used to make our brain. If we have too much omega-6 or, more precisely, if our mother did when we were in vitro, studies have shown a degree of impairment greater than if the developing embryo were exposed to lead. We no longer use leaded petrol for exactly that reason, but apparently it's fine to expose mothers and babies to something worse and encourage them to spread it on their toast in the morning.

11. Polyunsaturated fats degrade a man's ability to have children

Sperm counts are dropping rapidly in all Western countries. In Israel, one of the world's highest consumers of polyunsaturated fats, the situation is so dire that finding a man who's capable of reproducing is likely to be almost impossible by 2030. A sperm count is an old-fashioned but still highly reliable way of measuring a man's reproductive potency. In 1992, researchers from the University of Copenhagen published a study of sperm quality trends over the preceding half-century. After reviewing 61 trials, the scientists came to the shocking conclusion that the average sperm count had halved in just 50 years. Similar numbers and rates of decline are now being reported in all Western countries (although alarmingly, at 3 per cent drop per annum, Australia is at the high end).

We've known for some time that in experimental animals, high omega-6 fat consumption lowers sperm count and significantly impairs the quality of the remaining sperm. A 2009 study in humans has taken that research one step further, where 82 infertile men were compared with 78 proven fertile men. Detailed profiles of the fatty-acid make-up of each man's blood plasma were prepared. The results were unequivocal. Infertile men had a significantly higher ratio of omega-6 to omega-3 (15:1 versus 6:1 in fertile men). Critically, the higher the omega-6, the lower the sperm count.

> **There are many good reasons not to consume seed oils, but I reckon the future of the human race probably tops the list.**

There are many good reasons not to consume seed oils, but I reckon the future of the human race probably tops the list. Food companies are doing nothing less than committing biochemical genocide by filling every food we eat with omega-6 fats. We're having our reproductive capacity disabled en masse, and far from protesting against it, our health authorities are actively encouraging us to consume more.

And we don't even need to eat them to suffer

While the MDA and 4-HNE we make ourselves from consuming too much omega-6 are devastating enough, it's now becoming abundantly clear that we can make seed oils even more dangerous. All we need to do is heat them before we eat them.

A study released in 2014 found that when seed oils containing omega-6 fats were heated at a normal deep-frying, roasting or baking temperature (180°C), they created significant quantities of MDA and 4-HNE, among other highly toxic chemicals. Each time the oil was re-used, the concentration jumped significantly. The study showed that by the fifth oil re-use, it had five times the concentration of these chemicals as on the first, which was already alarmingly high.

We directly ingest these pre-made cancer bombs every time we eat a food cooked in those oils (for example, anything fried in seed oil) or that used heated fats in the recipe (for example, baked goods). They're even lurking in products sold cold but made using heated oils (such as margarines).

Worse than that, the researchers also made the point that all they could measure was the amount of these chemicals left in the oil. Since they're highly volatile, they're constantly escaping into the air around us when the food is being cooked and when it's being eaten. It's likely that this explains the stubbornly high rates of lung cancer among women in Asian countries, where smoking is rare among women, but wok-frying with canola oil is a daily task.

According to the Australian Institute of Health and Welfare (AIHW), almost 48,000 Australians died from cancer in 2017. Despite huge advances in treatment, it's still the second biggest cause of death in Australia. Their most recent report reveals that between 1982 and 2015, the incidence of all cancers in Australia grew by an alarming 27 per cent. In 2003, 274 Australians were diagnosed per day. In 2018, it was 379 people. Per day!

And it isn't just cancer. In countries exposed to the Western diet for most of the past five decades, the number of new cases of multiple sclerosis recorded per year (after adjusting for population increases) has quadrupled and the numbers of people with other diseases associated with these lethal chemicals has also been pushing steadily higher.

Prevention is clearly the key to changing a future full of untimely death from horrible chronic disease. Unfortunately, those charged with advising us are blind to the real cause of these lethal epidemics. Worse than that, they're frequently the people responsible for us consuming the oils in the first place. McDonald's, for example, switched from frying in beef fat to canola oil in 2004 after incessant pressure from the Heart Foundation. KFC followed suit in 2012, switching from palm oil to canola. And it's not just the big names. Rest assured, almost everybody now selling fried food (from the corner takeaway right through to the most expensive restaurant) will be frying it in the cheapest vegetable (seed) oil they can find.

2

Identifying polyunsaturated fats

When I first concluded that seed oils were a lethal part of my family's diet, I headed for the pantry to see how much of the stuff there really was in our food. I was in for a shock. Our bread contained canola oil. Our mayonnaise was based on sunflower oil. The savoury crackers we were including in lunch boxes were made with a mix of canola and palm oil. The puff pastry Lizzie used to make apple pie was made with margarine. And the fish and chips we had on a Friday night was cooked in cottonseed oil by the local (well-intentioned) fish and chipper. Even the fish fingers I occasionally pan-fried as a treat for the twins were full of canola oil. A quick back-of-the-envelope calculation told me that even on our minimally processed, fructose-free diet, we were still consuming dangerous quantities of seed oil.

As strange as it might sound, avoiding seed oils is significantly more difficult than avoiding sugar. At least we can taste sugar. If a food tastes sweet, it either contains sugar or an artificial sweetener, so even if we can't see a label (because we're in a restaurant, say), we've got a fair old clue that the food might be a problem. But we can't taste polyunsaturated fats. To our tastebuds, once it's in a processed food, a fat is a fat. We have no way of knowing by taste or consistency whether the fat is polyunsaturated or not. And much of the time, food manufacturers don't help. As a minimum, they must indicate how much of the fat in a product is saturated because all healthy-eating messaging is focused on saturated fat, but this is often all they will tell us, leaving us completely in the dark as to how much of the fat is polyunsaturated. I scoured the supermarket shelves for many hundreds of hours to determine the safest options (ones that were fructose-free and seed-oil-free) for my family. In some food categories, it was just not possible to find any safe options at all, leaving DIY as the only choice. The sections that follow are the results of my detective hunt for foods that are low in both added fructose and added seed oils.

We have no way of knowing by taste or consistency whether the fat is polyunsaturated or not.

Our bodies can make only two kinds of fat: saturated and monounsaturated. This is why 92 per cent of the fat in our bodies is one or the other of those two types. The other 8 per cent should be fats based on the polyunsaturated fats we get from our diet, the so-called 'essential fatty acids' (essential because we need them and we can't make them). The two main polyunsaturated fatty acids our bodies can't manufacture are linoleic acid (LA, an omega-6 fatty acid) and alpha-linolenic acid (ALA, an omega-3 fatty acid). We need them to manufacture other types of polyunsaturated fats, the hormone-like molecules we use to control many of our systems (mainly inflammation and immunity), as critical components of our eyes and as messengers in our central nervous system. But we only need a maximum of 3 per cent, and perhaps as little as 1 per cent, of the calories we consume to be made up of these essential fatty acids. As with most things in our bodies, we need the balance to be just right. If we have just the right amount of both, then everything hums along. But if we push out the balance between them or have too many of them in total, we start to encounter the problems set out in the previous chapters.

Omega-3 and omega-6 fatty acids

The science is not definitive on this, but it looks like we need to eat about 1.5 grams of omega-3 ALA and a similar amount of omega-6 LA a day. I say it's not definitive because there are examples of populations who have survived on much less than this and researchers are not certain that they know all the things that our bodies use these fats for. What they do know is that before the invention of agriculture and the introduction of processed seed-based foods into our diet, we probably consumed polyunsaturated fats in the ratio of one omega-6 to one omega-3, and the total consumption of each was in the 1.5 grams per day ballpark. But for the 10,000 or so years between the invention of agriculture and the beginning of the Industrial Revolution, we appear to have been getting by on a ratio of about two omega-6 to one omega-3 with no significant ill effects. This change occurred because grains are a source of omega-6 and so our consumption increased as we began to use grain-based flours in our diets.

Prior to the invention of seed oils, we obtained omega-3 and omega-6 from our everyday diet without any great difficulty because just about every whole food contains some of each. Grains and nuts (and the flesh of animals that eat them) are higher in omega-6 fats, while grasses and algae (and the flesh of animals that eat them) are higher in omega-3 fats. While you could easily get more than enough by subsisting on nuts (or lamb chops), there's really no need to especially seek out these fats.

Now that seed oils are used in just about every commercially produced food, the amount of omega-6 oils we consume has exploded.

Now that seed oils are used in just about every commercially produced food, the amount of omega-6 oils we consume has exploded. We would obtain almost twice our daily requirement from just one medium serve of McDonalds fries (2.8 grams). We would also get our daily requirement of omega-3 fat (1.5 grams) from the same serving. While most of us are probably getting just enough omega-3 ALA, we're all getting vast amounts of omega-6 LA if we eat polyunsaturated seed oils or anything made with them – which is an awful lot of things.

Reliable surveys on fatty-acid consumption are pretty thin on the ground in Australia, but based on recent data from the UK, we are probably hovering around a ratio of 20 omega-6 to one omega-3 (or ten times the ratio of 200 years ago).

The reason the amount of omega-6 we're consuming has become so large so quickly is pretty simple. The animal fats we eat are being progressively replaced with cheaper (and 'healthier') seed oils. If we're to avoid overconsuming polyunsaturated fats, we need to get very good at knowing where they will be located in our weekly shop.

HOW MUCH POLYUNSATURATED FAT SHOULD WE EAT?

We need 1.5 grams of omega-3 and 1.5 grams of omega-6 per day. There's no evidence of harm at double those quantities and there's also no evidence of harm even if we are having twice as much omega-6 as omega-3. So, the rule of thumb I am using is that we should be aiming for polyunsaturated fat consumption to be between 3 and 6 grams per day.

The supermarket

The following section sets out a guided tour of the polyunsaturated-fat landmines hidden in the aisles of your local supermarket. I have listed commonly available products that publish detailed information about their fat and sugar content, but if you don't see your product in the list, flip to 'How to read a label' on page 74.

Raw fats

Identifying which products contain polyunsaturated oils is a difficult job. Manufacturers are only required to label the total fat content, and the presence of saturated fats and trans fats. They do not need to identify the monounsaturated or polyunsaturated-fat contents unless they make a front-of-pack health claim about the presence of polyunsaturated fats. The task is made even trickier by the fact that we can't taste the difference between a saturated and a polyunsaturated fat.

As you wander down the cooking-oil aisle at your local supermarket, you won't find anything labelled 'Polyunsaturated Oil' or 'Seed Oil'. What you will see is a dizzying array of 'Cooking Oil' labels. To avoid oils that are high in easily oxidised polyunsaturated fats, steer well clear of those produced by crushing seeds and opt instead for those ones pressed from tropical fruits or some nuts – for example, coconut, avocado, olive or macadamia. The best fats of all, however, will be found in the fridge section rather than the cooking-oil aisle. That's where you'll discover lard, dripping, ghee and butter.

Use	Use with Caution	Don't Use
• Olive oil	• Hazelnut oil	• Canola (rapeseed) oil
• Coconut oil	• Cashew oil	• Sunflower oil
• Avocado oil	• Almond oil	• Safflower oil
• Sustainable palm oil and palm kernel oil	• Peanut oil	• Soybean (soy) oil
	• Pistachio oil	• Rice bran oil
	• Flaxseed (linseed) oil	• Corn oil
• High oleic sunflower oil (see page 50)		• Grapeseed oil
		• Cottonseed oil
• Macadamia oil		• Sesame seed oil
• Chestnut oil		• Pumpkin seed oil
• Butter		• Other nut oils (including walnut, pecan, pine, brazil, etc.)
• Ghee		
• Animal fat (including lard, tallow, fowl, etc.)		

The criterion for which column an oil or fat appears in is the amount of omega-6 fatty acids it contains. The oils in the middle are rated 'Use with Caution', largely because they contain borderline large-ish amounts of omega-6 (except for flaxseed/linseed oil, which is there just because it contains a large amount of polyunsaturated fats). This means that if one of these oils is a staple in your daily cooking, you should consider switching to one from the 'use' column, but if you use them only occasionally, they're fine to keep.

DOES IT MATTER WHETHER MY OIL IS A VIRGIN?

You'll come across some interesting terms on the front of a bottle of oil. In Australia and New Zealand, there are no mandatory standards for front-of-pack labelling of oils, but the olive-oil industry has a voluntary code which is in line with international labelling standards, and some other oils choose to make use of this code too. Here's what the labels mean:

Virgin means that no heat or chemicals have been used to extract the oil from the fruit. Instead, the fruit has been crushed into a paste and spun, just like a washing machine on spin cycle, to separate the oil from everything else.

For olive oils, virgin means that the free fatty-acid content (a measure of quality, where lower is better) is less than 2 per cent. For coconut oils, it means that the oil is obtained from fresh, mature coconut kernels through means which do not lead to alteration of the oil. The free fatty-acid content should be less than 0.5 per cent. Ninety per cent of the world's coconut-oil producers have agreed to adhere to this standard. Olive-oil producers claim to adhere to it, but testing reveals that they don't always.

Extra virgin is virgin oil that is judged to have a superior taste. For olive oils, this means the free fatty-acid content must be lower than 0.8 per cent. While you might see 'extra virgin' on a bottle of coconut oil, there is no standard definition of that term for coconut oil; in this case, read it as 'virgin'.

Cold-pressed or first cold pressing means that the oil was extracted using a traditional hydraulic press without the use of chemicals. If the oil was obtained by any other method, it should not say anything about 'pressing' on the label. The 'cold' simply means that it was not heated. In other words, the pressing was done at room temperature (which means less than 27°C for olive oils). By the way, there is no second press of an oil, so 'first press' is really a meaningless description. Increasingly, industrial oils are being labelled this way as well as olive and coconut oils. It is meaningless when it comes to the polyunsaturated fat content of the product.

Refined is not often written on the front of the pack. This is the oil that didn't make the cut as either virgin or extra virgin because of its free-fatty-acid content. It has been further refined using chemical and physical filters to lower the free-fatty-acid content (to less than 0.3 per cent). The result is an oil that is very light in colour and tasteless. Refined oil is not nutritionally worse for you than virgin oil, but if you have an aversion to food that's been chemically treated then leave 'refined', 'pure' and 'light' (or 'extra light') oils alone. When you see an oil on the list of ingredients of a processed food, it is likely to be refined oil because it does not introduce a new taste into the end product.

Pure or no description means the oil is not virgin. It is usually a blend of virgin and refined oils. Pure olive oil is a blend of refined olive oil, and so not entitled to be labelled as virgin.

Light or extra light is only used on olive oil and means the oil tastes less like olives. Light means light on taste (and usually colour), not calories. The 'lightness' is usually achieved by blending olive oil with refined olive oil. The 'lighter' the oil, the greater the proportion of refined oil it contains.

Be careful with oil from palms

Because of their high saturated-fat content, palm oils are pretty good from a biochemical perspective, but in order to grow the palms, large tracts of native forest are being destroyed. Indonesia and Malaysia produce almost 90 per cent of the palm oils used in the world today. The amount of land dedicated to oil production in those two countries has tripled since 1995. The last surviving members of several endangered species, including orangutans, live in the old-growth forests being cut down for palm plantations. If the market continues to grow at its current rate, it's likely that these species will be extinct within 20 years. And that's reason enough for me to avoid palm-oil-based products.

There is a movement among many processed-food manufacturers to insist on sustainably produced palm oils, but the reality is that, at the moment, the amount of sustainable palm-oil production is insignificant.

Cooking-oil products

Food manufacturers don't always stick to the standardised labels I've used in the box above. You never know: you might encounter a 'nut- and seed-oil blend' when next you shop, or perhaps a 'porpoise-tear-infused Mediterranean healthy cooking oil'! Behind all that marketing guff, Australian foods are required to display the fat breakdown of the product, describing, at least, how much of the fat is saturated. Look at the nutrition information panel on the back of the product under the heading 'Fats'. Scroll down to the line that says 'Polyunsaturated' and across to the column that says 'per 100 ml' or 'per 100 g'. If the number in that column is greater than 13, put it back on the shelf.

Because the amount of polyunsaturated fats in a product is currently perceived as a marketing benefit, most products that are high in these fats will clearly state the amount they contain. Ironically, it is only the products low in polyunsaturates (like lard, ghee and animal fats) that don't clearly state the amount on the label.

'Smoke point'

Not all fats and oils (even the good ones) are good for cooking all things. When any fat is heated past a certain temperature, called its 'smoke point', it produces an acrid smoke. As the oil heats past that point, the free fatty acids increase dramatically and the taste of the fat degrades. The more free fatty acids there are, the lower the smoke point. This means that if you re-use oils, each time you heat them, the smoke point becomes progressively lower. An old oil smokes more easily than a new oil. If the oil or fat you are using is smoking, turn down the temperature straight away and consider using a different fat for the job.

In this table, I've set out the typical smoke points for oils you might be using. Remember that these are rough numbers as each brand will get a slightly different result, but the table should enable you to figure out the best oil to use for various types of cooking. In a nutshell, all of these oils and fats can be used for pan-frying. However, butter should not be used for deep-frying.

SMOKE POINTS OF GOOD FATS AND OILS			
Temperature (°C/°F)	Fat or oil	Oven temperature	Cooking style
270/518	Refined avocado oil	Very hot	Pan-fry, wok-fry, deep-fry, use in oven
250/482	Ghee		
240/464	Extra light olive oil		
230/446	Palm oil Refined coconut oil		
220/428	Tallow (beef fat)		
210/410	Macadamia oil	Hot	
205/401	Extra virgin olive oil		
200/193	Virgin olive oil Virgin avocado oil		
190/374	Lard (pig fat)	Moderate	Deep-fry (up to 190°C/374°F)
175/347	Extra virgin coconut oil		Pan-fry or work-fry (up to 175°C/347°F)
150–170/302–308	Butter	Low	

From a nutrition perspective, the only really sensible choice is butter, although if you want to go old-school, you could use lard or dripping.

Spreads

Most of us like to spread a little fat on our bread. From a nutrition perspective, the only really sensible choice is butter, although if you want to go old-school, you could use lard or dripping.

The only problem is that spreading butter that's been in the fridge is like attempting to shave a lump of concrete. The good news is that you don't need to store butter in the fridge all the time. All fats go rancid or oxidise if left exposed to oxygen for long enough at a high enough temperature. Polyunsaturated fats like those that dominate the seed oils in margarines react rapidly with oxygen when left at room temperature, but because of its high saturated-fat content, butter is much more tolerant of being stored out of the fridge.

Unfortunately, in Australia 'room temperature' can vary greatly, depending on where you live. Butter is rock-hard at fridge temperature (4°C), softens to an almost spreadable consistency at about 15°C, is nicely spreadable at a European (or Brisbane winter) room temperature of about 23°C and is a pourable liquid at 33°C, which is the temperature on a balmy summer's day in the north. If you live anywhere south of Brisbane, for most of the year you will get away with leaving your butter on the counter for up to a week without it going rancid. Salted butter will last much better than unsalted butter because of the preservative effect of the salt. You'll be able to tell when the butter has started to turn because the outside will be a darker colour than the inside and it will start to smell and taste unpleasant.

Eating rancid butter won't hurt you but I wouldn't recommend it as a hobby.

There are a few solutions to the spreadability problem. Simply get good at judging consumption so that you only ever have a week's worth of butter on the counter, or become organised enough to put the butter in the fridge overnight and pull it out for use an hour before you need it. Or make sure your toast is hot when you drop on a chunk carved from the block. Or fork out the big bucks for spreadable butter.

The only brand of spreadable butter available in Australia is Mainland Buttersoft. Like normal butter, it contains nothing but cream and salt. It is more spreadable than butter (although only about half as spreadable as margarine) because some of the harder saturated fatty acids have been removed. It is nutritionally equivalent to butter and there is no downside to using it, other than the price.

A so-called 'dairy blend' is not butter (no matter how many times it says 'made with real butter' or some such on the front of the pack). Blends are an attempt to overcome the spreadability issue by mixing butter and margarine together. If the ingredient list on an item is anything other than cream and salt, it's not butter – it probably contains seed oils and should be put back on the shelf.

Olive-oil margarines might look like a good idea because olive oil is a perfectly acceptable cooking option, but because its melting point is -40° C, olive oil can't be made into a solid margarine. So, no matter how many pictures of olives appear on the front of that olive oil spread, it is a blend of olive oil and seed oils – and usually only about one-third of the oil used is from olives. Put it back on the shelf.

READING THE LABEL

In Australia, a manufacturer needs to provide no more detail on a label about the oil used than the words 'vegetable oil' in the list of ingredients. What they mean is 'seed oils', 'nut oils' or 'tropical fruit oils', but they're not required to spell that out. Vegetable oil on the label could be anything in the packet, but if it's canola oil, which is usually more expensive and considered 'healthy', they'll generally make a bit of a song and dance about it. If the product says it is low in saturated fat and contains 'vegetable oil', it's probably canola oil. If the product contains olive oil, the manufacturer will definitely say so. It's so (relatively) expensive they'll want you to know it's there. If the product contains soy oil, they'll usually say 'vegetable oil (contains antioxidants)' or something similar.

Margarine-makers feel the seed basis of their product is a selling feature, so they'll often say which oil is used (often a blend of canola and sunflower). All are extremely bad choices. If the label just says 'vegetable oil' assume the worst – that it's soy or sunflower oil – and avoid it.

Breads

If you're buying butter, you'll probably want something to spread it on. Most supermarket breads now include vegetable oil rather than the more traditional lard, and it's usually – by the look of the antioxidant claims – soy oil or (sometimes) canola. The bad news is that most commercial breads contain seed oils. The good news is that it is rarely very much and, if you want to avoid it altogether, there are some reasonable alternatives available. In the table over the page, I've listed the most popular supermarket brands ranked by oil content. And just so sugar doesn't sneak under the radar, I've also taken that into account. The better choices have the sugar content under 3 grams per 100 grams and, of course, the polyunsaturated-fat content as low as possible.

If white, wholemeal or multigrain is not your style, the best non-white bread is Burgen Rye, but bear in mind that you will be doubling the amount of polyunsaturated fat you consume from bread. If bread is a major part of your diet and the rest of your diet is pushing the boundaries on your daily polyunsaturated-fat allowance, then an effective way to cut back might be to switch to one of the breads in the left or middle column. Of course, if the only bread you eat is a couple of slices of Burgen Rye toast in the morning, then the difference will not be significant. Sourdough bread does not usually include fat or sugar, so if you are in doubt, go for that. As a general rule, even the supermarket brands of fresh-baked sourdough are free of added sugar and seed oils, but it's always worth a quick check of the label before you drop it in your trolley. The same goes for the rapidly increasing range of supermarket

Sourdough bread does not usually include fat or sugar, so if you are in doubt, go for that.

artisan European-style breads. Our current favourite is Aldi's Pane di Casa white loaf, which has no added oils or sugar, but there are similar options available from both Coles and Woolworths.

Popular supermarket breads: based on sugar and polyunsaturated-fat content

Use	Use with Caution	Don't Use
• **Sourdoughs** • **European-style breads (but check ingredients)**	• Coles White and Bakery White • Woolworths White, Wholemeal and Country Loaf White • Tip Top® Sunblest® White, Wholemeal and Multigrain	• Most other breads (usually because of the sugar content)

Buying your bread from a bakery will not help you avoid seed oils unless you go for the European varieties. Baker's Delight, for example, uses canola oil and soy flour in most of their standard white-bread products (we know this because they publish detailed nutritional information). It is only once you venture into their sourdough or European-style loaves that these ingredients disappear from the list. The best way to know what your local baker is using is to ask. Most of them are up at 3 am adding the oil to the mix, so they'll have a pretty good idea what they're using and some are quite happy to change it. Our local Brumby's does us an order of 30 hamburger rolls (for school lunches) made with olive oil every week.

Wraps

If wraps are more your speed, the good news is that it is much easier to find wraps with no added oils. None of the Mountain

Bread wraps use any oil. The polyunsaturated-fat content comes exclusively from the flour and the best choice, rye, contains just 0.7 grams per 100 grams (two wraps). Sugar is not added to Mountain Bread so the sugars are from the flours alone and almost all are less than 3 grams per 100 grams. The other major brands (Coles, Woolworths, Mission and Tip Top) add palm oil and sugar. If you are not concerned about the sustainability aspects of palm oil, you can find some varieties of these brands with sugar content of less than 3 grams per 100 grams. Rice and corn are gluten-free grains, so wraps which list only rice or corn flour in the ingredients are a good choice for folks watching out for gluten.

Flour

Bread made without oils of any kind will still contain polyunsaturated-fat content from the flour. Most are sufficiently low as to be largely irrelevant but if you eat a lot of bread then avoid the soy-flour-based breads altogether and be careful with ones made from the flours listed in the middle column below. You would need to eat a whole loaf of white sandwich bread (600 grams or eighteen slices) to blow your maximum daily allowance of 6 grams of polyunsaturated fat if you choose only breads made from the flours in the left column.

Use	Use with Caution	Don't Use
• **Potato**	• Rye (dark)	• Reduced-fat soy
• **White rice**	• Wholemeal wheat	• Soy
• **Wheat**	• Spelt	
• **Rye (light)**	• Corn	
• **Barley**		

DIY

Of course, the best way to ensure you know exactly what's in your bread is to make it yourself. This has the twin benefits of ensuring it doesn't contain sugar or seed oil.

Until I actually gave it a go, bread-making seemed like a bridge (way) too far, no matter how many diseases I was avoiding. But know this: it isn't that hard, even without a bread-making machine. Using the recipes in Chapter 3, it really is quite simple to whip up a loaf of fresh sourdough or other crusty bread every morning. Yes, every morning! And, into the bargain, you might find yourself appreciating the bread a little more and so eating less of it, which is also likely to do you good.

Other spreads

Avoiding sugar will already have left your pantry pretty bare in the spreads department. You will have chucked out the honey, jam and Nutella, but you might still have a jar of peanut butter (or other nut butter) and some Vegemite on hand. Vegemite contains no added oils and very little sugar so you can hang onto that. 'Butters' made from seeds and nuts are a trickier proposition. Seeds and nuts are not a critical part of our diet and should be consumed sparingly (especially seeds). If you treat seeds as a garnish and nuts as an occasional treat, you won't go wrong. The graph below sets out how much of a given seed or nut you'd need to eat to reach my suggested maximum daily amount of polyunsaturated fat (6 grams).

For a sense of scale, I've included butter. I like buttery toast but even I'd be pushing it to knock off 200 grams in a day. You'll do your daily polyunsaturated-fat budget (assuming you eat nothing else with polyunsaturated fat) with three walnuts, 70 pistachios or a little over half a cup of cashews, but you could have four cups of macadamias.

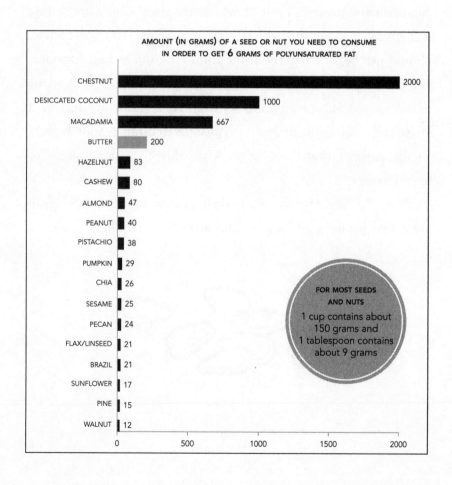

AMOUNT (IN GRAMS) OF A SEED OR NUT YOU NEED TO CONSUME IN ORDER TO GET **6** GRAMS OF POLYUNSATURATED FAT

CHESTNUT	2000
DESICCATED COCONUT	1000
MACADAMIA	667
BUTTER	200
HAZELNUT	83
CASHEW	80
ALMOND	47
PEANUT	40
PISTACHIO	38
PUMPKIN	29
CHIA	26
SESAME	25
PECAN	24
FLAX/LINSEED	21
BRAZIL	21
SUNFLOWER	17
PINE	15
WALNUT	12

FOR MOST SEEDS AND NUTS
1 cup contains about 150 grams and 1 tablespoon contains about 9 grams

'Butters' made from any of these nuts obviously contain similar amounts of polyunsaturated fat per gram. A cup of nut butter contains 260 grams and a tablespoon holds a little over 15 grams. So just three tablespoons of peanut or almond butter or five of cashew butter will have you hitting your daily limit.

There is much less polyunsaturated fat in Sanitarium peanut butter products than you might expect, and this is likely because they don't start from raw peanuts. Rather, some commercial peanut butter is made from peanut flour that has been partially de-fatted. This lowers the total fat of the product and increases the protein, both of which are good if you are selling a high-fat product to a fat-wary consumer. You, of course, should not be worried about the total fat content but, for once, the public paranoia about fat works in favour of those of us avoiding polyunsaturated fats as well. As a result, we receive a reasonable selection of low-polyunsaturated-fat peanut butters in the supermarket, leaving us with only the added sugar to worry about.

If you'd like to make your own peanut butter, simply grab some raw peanuts, add a splash of peanut oil and blend.

Condiments

If you are avoiding sugar, you will already have given most condiments the flick, since sugar is the primary ingredient in just about every 'savoury' sauce, and adding a condiment is the dietary equivalent of adding chocolate sauce to everything. Indeed, chocolate sauce would often contain less sugar.

Some condiments, however, might still remain in your pantry because they have an acceptable sugar content. Let's have a look at those.

Mayonnaise and pesto

Don't buy low-fat mayonnaise. They are padded with copious quantities of sugar. Most of the big-brand full-fat mayos are also not an option as they are made from sunflower oil, one of the nastiest seed oils. There are a few exceptions, such as Good Fat Mayo from the Undivided Food Co., but they are not cheap. Of course, you could just make your own. There are about a million recipes for olive-oil mayo on the web and just to save you click-time, I've included my favourite in Chapter 3. It takes less than a minute to make and lasts a week in the fridge.

Unfortunately, commercial mayo is used as the basis for commercial coleslaw, so you can expect a big serve of sugar and seed oil if you buy pre-made coleslaw from the supermarket. Besides, making your own with the kids is good fun (seriously). Just chop up a cabbage of your choice, mix in some grated carrot, then stir in (this is where the kids come in – using their hands) a lump of homemade mayo, and Bob's your uncle. I defy you or your friends to detect the difference, but it's added-sugar free and, if you've made your own mayo or shopped in the premium aisle, it's also seed-oil free.

Most commercial pestos and dips (and dip-like substances such as tzatziki and hummus) are made using a seed oil (usually canola or sunflower) as the base. For straight tomato or basil pesto, sunflower oil is usually the primary ingredient. Unfortunately, almost none of them publish the polyunsaturated-fat content of the product, but given the ingredients, there are very few good options. Tzatziki sauces are low in fat (and therefore polyunsaturates) but high in sugar and the rest are very high in poyunsaturated fats, even if they are sometimes quite low in sugar. Fortunately, most of the basic sauces and pestos have been handmade using olive oil for generations and there is no shortage of recipes for doing it yourself. Lizzie has tested a large number of these and collected the best and the easiest to make in Chapter 3. You still need to be careful with some of the ingredients, however. We've found it very difficult to get sundried tomatoes that are not sold in seed oil (usually sunflower), but they do exist. Look for the Greenland brand (little vacuum-sealed packs in the refrigerated deli section rather than with the jars). You can also buy them dry, without oil, and simply add your own olive oil. You can play with these basic recipes according to your own taste, but do remember to check the label of any pickled or bottled vegetable you'd like to use to make sure it doesn't list a seed oil (or 'vegetable oil') in the ingredient list.

Salad dressings

You're going to need to get used to eating salads au naturel or with homemade dressings by the look of the following table.

Some brands have absolutely no fat and therefore no polyunsaturated fat. But every serving (20 grams) will deliver a big lump of sugar (at least half and usually a whole teaspoon's worth). If you want no sugar, get ready for a huge serve of polyunsaturated fat instead. All of the dressings that contain fat are based on sunflower, rice bran, canola or soybean oil, and pretty much all of the polyunsaturated fat numbers are pretty ugly. If you cannot get through the day without salad dressing, your best choice is probably the Praise Italian 100% Fat Free. It will still give you half a teaspoon of sugar in a single serve, but if you only have one serve and that's all the sugar you are consuming that day, it's not going to kill you. The dressings listed in the Use with Caution column

Commercial salad dressings: based on sugar and polyunsaturated-fat contents

Use	Use with Caution	Don't Use
• Homemade	• Paul Newman's Own Light Balsamic Vinaigrette and Classic Balsamic Vinaigrette • Praise Fat-Free Balsamic, Balsamic, French, Greek and Italian • Coles Caesar • Birch & Waite Balsamic, Greek-Style and Caesar	• Most other commercial dressings

all contain around 2 grams of polyunsaturated fat and between 0.5 and 2 grams of sugar per 20 gram serve. Once again, making your own is the best option. Luckily, it's pretty quick and easy (see page 135).

Cracker biscuits

If you're staying away from sugar, you won't be eating most sweet biscuits, but even cracker biscuits are full of vegetable oils. In the chart below, I've set out the cracker biscuits that publish their polyunsaturated-fat content. Many don't provide this information and most of these are likely to be cooked in a blend of canola and palm oil, so should be avoided anyway. Peckish brand explicitly say they are cooked in rice bran oil and so should be avoided.

Cracker biscuits: based on published sugar and polyunsaturated-fat content

Use	Use with Caution	Don't Use
• **Arnott's Rice, Rye and Corn Cruskits** • **Arnott's Salada 97% Fat-free Multigrain, Wholemeal and Light Original**	• Arnott's Vita-Weat Original and Superfoods Ancient Grains and Seeds • Arnott's Salada Original	• Arnott's Light Cruskits (because of the sugar content) • All other varieties of Arnott's Vita-Weat • Sakata Authentic Wholegrain • Peckish • Most other crackers

For once, a gluten-free product is at the right end of the scale. San-J Tamari Brown Rice Crackers have no seed oils or sugar added and, although they don't publish an exact breakdown of their polyunsaturated fat content, they are likely to be very similar to the products on the left side of the graph. Rye or Corn Cruskits and Multigrain, Wholemeal or Light Salada are also good cracker-biscuit options. They are very low in sugar and also hover around the 1 gram per 100 gram mark for polyunsaturated-fat content. One hundred grams is 17.5 Cruskits or six Saladas, so unless you are feeling really peckish, you won't be putting a serious dent in your polyunsaturated-fat budget by making a snack based on either of these. They don't publish their polyunsaturated-fat content but based on the rest of the fat profile and the ingredients list, water crackers would be fine too.

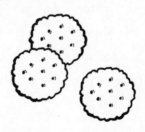

Potato crisps and corn chips

Australian crisps are generally fried in either sunflower or palm oil. You might assume, as I did, that the palm-oil option is the way to go from a nutritional perspective, but you'd be wrong. The sunflower oil being used is not the stuff you can buy on the shelf in the supermarket, it's the oil from a type of sunflower bred to produce seed oils that are extremely low in polyunsaturated fats.

There is a large variation in the total fat content of crisps. Some have about the same amount of total fat as hot chips (around 20 grams per 100 grams), while others have almost double that. Because the total fat varies a lot, so does the amount of polyunsaturated fat, regardless of what oil was used to cook the chips.

HIGH OLEIC SUNFLOWER OIL

As the anti-animal-fat craze took hold in the 1980s, crisp manufacturers switched to soybean oils so they could claim their products were cooked 'in vegetable oil'. The problem with this is that seed oils need to be hydrogenated before they can be used for industrial frying, and hydrogenation creates significant percentages of trans fats.

During the 1990s, awareness of the dangers of trans fats was growing and producers needed to switch to an oil that still allowed them to claim 'vegetable oil' status but did not need to be hydrogenated. Olive oil was too expensive, which left palm oil as the only real option. However, there was nowhere near enough palm oil to supply all the producers then using soybean oil. But a solution was at hand. Russian scientists had successfully created a mutant species of sunflower that produced oil very high in monounsaturated fats and very low in polyunsaturates, just like olive oil. Oleic acid is the primary monounsaturated fat in this sunflower oil (and in olive oil), so they named it high oleic sunflower oil.

When you see 'sunflower oil' on a crisp packet, it generally means high oleic sunflower oil. Crisps are the only supermarket product where you're likely to encounter this type of oil.

Popular supermarket crisps and corn chips: based on polyunsaturated-fat content

Use	Use with Caution	Don't Use
• **Red Rock Deli Salted Potato Chips** • **Woolworths Deli Style**	• Woolworths Corn Chips • Byron Bay Chilli Co Corn Chips • Coles Corn Chips • Smiths Extra Crunchy • Doritos Original Corn Chips • Macro Organic Corn Chips • Coles Gluten Free Corn Chips • Woolworths Original Stacked • Smiths Thinly Cut • Kettle • Smiths Original	• Tyrells Chips • Coles Stacked • Coles Crinkle Cut • Tostitos Tortilla Chips • Thins • CC's Original Corn Chips • Pringles • Natural Chip Co. • French Fries Original • Woolworths Crinkle Cut

In the table above, I've set out the major brands of crisps and corn chips. To keep it simple, I've just included the plain salted ones. Flavoured varieties are usually identical when it comes to polyunsaturated-fat content, but flavouring often significantly increases the sugar content (which is almost zero in plain salted chips), so be careful. The Red Rock Deli Salted Potato Chips come out as the best choice because they have the lowest amount of total fat (22.5 grams per 100). So, if crisps are your thing, stick to the choices on the left side of the table. One hundred grams of chips is quite a lot. The lunch-box size packs that come in big boxes of 20 (or so) weigh only 19 grams each (so they can claim to be only 100 calories) and probably represent a reasonable child-sized serve. Even if an adult ate two of those in a sitting, they would be consuming just half a gram (Red Rock) to 1.5 grams (Woolworths Crinkle Cut) of polyunsaturated fat.

Frozen vegetables

All frozen vegetables are fine. Eat as much of them as you can stand. The only exception is the one we barely regard as a vegetable, potato. And that's only really because of how it is cooked.

All frozen vegetables are fine. Eat as much of them as you can stand.

SWEET POTATO CHIPS

Don't be tempted by those healthy-sounding sweet potato chips (like McCain Sweet Potato Chips) that are now coming on to the market. Not only are they relatively high in polyunsaturated oils (at 1.5 grams per 100 grams), but they also have sugar added. A 100 gram serving of these little delights will provide you with 7.8 grams (almost 2 teaspoons) of sugar – in chips! Here's the ingredient list. Bet you weren't bargaining on finding peas in there.

Sweet potato (84%), batter (modified starches (1412, 1422), acidity regulators (450, 500), dextrin, natural colours (paprika, turmeric), molasses, pea fibre, rice flour, salt, sugar, thickener (415)), vegetable oil (contains one or more of the following oils: canola, cottonseed, soybean, sunflower, corn).

Frozen chips are marketed as 'oven-fry chips' but that's just anti-frying political correctness at play. They are exactly the same as the chips that Maccas and every chippie purveyor is slinging into their boiling seed oil. They're not seed-oil-free, as I'll explain in a moment, but they're acceptable if you actually do oven fry them or fry them in animal fat or olive oil.

Frozen chips are pieces of potato that have been dunked in a solution of dextrose and water (to help them brown more quickly and stop them sticking together in the bag), then pre-fried in seed oil. Obviously this is not ideal for us seed-oil avoiders but, because most of the fat is absorbed in the second frying, doing that final fry in animal fat means that we are significantly reducing the amount of polyunsaturated fat we eat as compared to getting the same thing from a shop or restaurant.

Not all frozen chips are cooked in the same seed oil, so by carefully reading the labels you can narrow your choices down to the least harmful ones.

Deep-frying the McCain Healthy Choice chips in animal fat will probably add about half a gram of polyunsaturated fat to the total (which brings it to 1.2 grams). While that total ends up being around half a gram of polyunsaturated fat more than if you went to the trouble of making the chips yourself, it is still an awfully long way short of the 4.2 grams you would get from 104 grams of McDonald's fries.

Commercial frozen chips: based on polyunsaturated-fat contents

Use	Use with Caution	Don't Use
• **McCain Healthy Choice Straight Cut** • **Coles Straight Cut** • **McCain Super-fries Steak Cut and Steak Cut**	• McCain Original Fries Crunchy Seasoned • Birds Eye Hot Chips Straight Cut • Woolworths Australian Chunky Steakhouse Chips • Birds Eye Golden Crunch Beer Batter Chips • Coles Chunky Wedges • Birds Eye Golden Crunch Beer Batter Steakhouse Chips • McCain Superfries Crinkle Cut • Birds Eye Golden Crunch Chips • Birds Eye Hot Chips Crinkles • McCain Beer Batter Chunky Cut • Coles Beer Batter Steakhouse Chips • Coles Crinkle Cut Chips • Birds Eye Golden Crunch Wedges	• Most other commercial frozen chips

Hash browns and other assorted frozen potato products

Perhaps you're partial to a fried-potato product with your bacon and eggs in the morning, and chips just wouldn't do. Unfortunately, the news is not good.

There are no good choices here. All commercial gems and hash browns hover around the 2 grams per 100 grams (about 1.25 hash browns) of polyunsaturated fat. This means that four frozen hash browns will blow your polyunsaturated fat limit for the day before you even go near the egg or the bacon. (And if you get them at Maccas, just three hash browns will push you over the edge.) If you really must have a hash brown with brekkie, keep it to one and make sure you stay away from the polyunsaturates for the rest of the day. The other alternative is, of course, to make your own. I've provided a dead-simple hash brown recipe in Chapter 3.

Frozen pizza

Most frozen pizzas have a similar oil content to takeaway pizzas but significantly more sugar. Most of this is added sugar in the pizza base and a higher-than-usual sugar content for the sauce. One 80-gram slice of the average supermarket frozen pizza will feed you about two teaspoons of sugar. If you're shopping for dinner in the freezer section, meat pies and sausage rolls (see opposite) are a far superior option. The seed oil is minimal, and most brands have barely any sugar. They rely on you adding the sugar via your trusty bottle of tomato sauce.

Rather than buying frozen pizzas, make your own – it's relatively easy to make a good pizza using unsweetened, un-oiled scone dough as the base (see Chapter 3) and the lowest-sugar tomato paste you can find. But be careful with the pastes – they vary enormously in sugar content. A thin smear of paste with any topping you like from your sugar-free cupboards and fridge will make a great, seed-oil-free and almost totally fructose-free meal.

If you can't come at making the dough yourself, McCain frozen pizza bases are a reasonable choice. They appear to contain very little polyunsaturated fat (less than 0.5 grams per base). If you restrict yourself to half a pizza using these bases, you won't go too far wrong. Gluten-free bases (for example, Silly Yaks) are also available in some supermarkets but their seed oil content is often three to four times as high. A little careful sleuthing will uncover some terrific alternatives such as those from Naturally Gluten Free, which are made from tapioca, rice and quinoa and have no added oil or sugar at all.

Frozen meat pies and sausage rolls

The classic Aussie pie is a very good option for low-sugar fans (unless you add sauce) and they're generally not bad from a poly-unsaturated-fat perspective either. Most pies and sausage rolls tend to use ingredients like beef tallow (rendered beef fat) and palm oil as well as some canola (in the pastry). And while the ingredient list for the pastry will often include 'margarine', this usually means cooking margarine, which is largely animal-fat based and contains less polyunsaturated fat than olive oil. On average, pies and sausage rolls end up having about 0.4 grams of polyunsaturated fat per 100 grams, which means a standard small (150 gram) pie contains 0.6 grams, and the average 700 gram family pie has 2.8 grams.

Added sugar varies quite a bit more than the fat content in pies and sausage rolls, so it's worth keeping an eye on. An average serving of one or two pieces (0.35 grams of polyunsaturated fat per piece) of a family pie is not going to put a serious hole in your daily polyunsaturated-fat budget. But if you normally eat a whole family pie yourself, you will want to dial that back a bit. The only real concern I have with pies is that they rarely contain much meat. The average label says that only about a quarter of the product is meat, and that meat is usually fairly vaguely described.

If you want to make sure that you have meat in your meat pies and that there is no added sugar or added polyunsaturated fat, you need to roll your own – which is easier than you might think. The recipe is in Chapter 3.

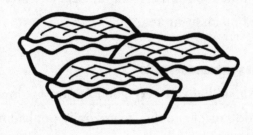

Frozen chicken and fish

Humanity cannot live on chips alone, so I've included some batter and crumbing recipes in Chapter 3. Just buy chicken or fish fillets and crumb or batter them up before dropping them in boiling animal fat – yum! If you have neither the time nor the inclination to get up to your elbows in batter or crumbing mix, there are some 'oven-fry' options in the freezer section of the supermarket. I don't really recommend any of them – even those lowest in polyunsaturated fat will put a fair old dent in your 6 gram per day allowance (containing between 3 and 9 grams of polyunsaturated fat per serve).

By way of comparison, 100 grams of McDonald's Chicken McNuggets (about six) is likely to contain around 5.5 grams of polyunsaturated fat. If you purchased some chicken-breast meat and crumbed or battered some 'nuggets', then deep-fried them in animal fat, they would contain about 1.2–1.5 grams of polyunsaturated fat. You'd be consuming around 4 grams less polyunsaturated fat than if you bought nuggets from Maccas, and 2.5–8 grams less than if you started from a box of frozen chicken(ish) product and deep-fried them in animal fat. You'd also have the advantage of knowing that your nugget was all breast chicken.

WHAT'S IN THAT BOX?

A typical box of crumbed or battered fish or chicken product often contains an awful lot less of the headline ingredient than you'd think. For example, here's the ingredients list for Steggles Crumbed Chicken Breast Fingers:

Chicken (38%), Water, Potato Flakes (6%) [Potato, Emulsifier (471), Mineral Salt (450), Preservative (223), Food Acid (330)], Wheat Flour, Rice Flour, Salt, Emulsifier (481), Dextrose, Spice Extracts (160c,100), Vegetable Oil (Cottonseed, Canola), Thickener (1404), Mineral Salts (450, 500, 451), Vegetable Gums (412, 415), Wheat Gluten, Wheat Starch, Tapioca Starch, Soy Protein, Dehydrated Vegetables (Onion, Garlic), Natural Flavour, Yeast Extract.

Fish is a little trickier than chicken because the meat itself can be high in polyunsaturated fats. Of the raw fish types, only Atlantic salmon and sardines contain significant quantities of polyunsaturated fat. Tropical fish like barramundi and hoki have almost no fat to speak of and flake has none. The products in the chart below are a representative sample from those companies that publish detailed fat content information.

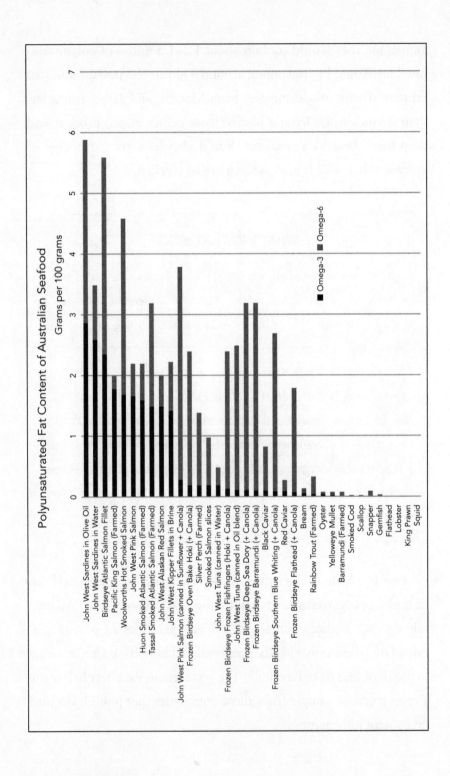

Polyunsaturated Fat Content of Australian Seafood
Grams per 100 grams

Omega-3
Omega-6

John West Sardines in Olive Oil
John West Sardines in Water
Birdseye Atlantic Salmon Fillet
Pacific King Salmon (Farmed)
Woolworths Hot Smoked Salmon
John West Pink Salmon
Huon Smoked Atlantic Salmon (Farmed)
Tassal Smoked Atlantic Salmon (Farmed)
John West Alaskan Red Salmon
John West Kipper Fillets in Brine
John West Pink Salmon (canned in Sunflower + Canola)
Frozen Birdseye Oven Bake Hoki (+ Canola)
Silver Perch (Farmed)
Smoked Salmon slices
John West Tuna (canned in Water)
Frozen Birdseye Frozen Fishfingers (Hoki + Canola)
John West Tuna (canned in Oil blend)
Frozen Birdseye Deep Sea Dory (+ Canola)
Frozen Birdseye Barramundi (+ Canola)
Black Caviar
Frozen Birdseye Southern Blue Whiting (+ Canola)
Red Caviar
Frozen Birdseye Flathead (+ Canola)
Bream
Rainbow Trout (Farmed)
Oyster
Yelloweye Mullet
Barramundi (Farmed)
Smoked Cod
Scallop
Snapper
Gemfish
Flathead
Lobster
King Prawn
Squid

Most fish products sold in the freezer section are made from hoki or flake, and most of them are crumbed and pre-fried in canola oil. Most of the polyunsaturated fat in those products is omega-6 from the oil and the soy flour that is generally used in the crumbing and batters. The obvious exception is any product that claims to be 100 per cent fish (such as the Birds Eye Natural Salmon Fillet).

Good options are tuna canned in water, fresh shellfish or fresh fillets of most other fish. If you are after fish and chips, once again, doing it yourself is the best way to minimise polyunsaturated fats, but remember that the average fillet is around 200 grams and after crumbing and frying will contain up to 5 grams of polyunsaturated fat. So, even the best fish meal will consume most of your daily allowance of polyunsaturated fats.

Since we've started frying our own fish and chips at home instead of buying them, three things have happened. We eat them less often (probably half as much as we used to) because it's just not as easy as reaching for the cash. When we do have them, it costs an awful lot less, and they taste an awful lot better! There's nothing quite so scrumptious as a chip (or crumbed breast fillet or battered piece of barra) freshly deep-fried in animal fat.

There's nothing quite so scrumptious as a chip (or crumbed breast fillet or battered piece of barra) freshly deep-fried in animal fat.

Beef

Even if we stay away from commercial fried foods, crisps, crackers, cereals, sauces and pastes, we'll still be getting more omega-6 than we should. This is because cattle are increasingly being fed on grains for the final months of their lives rather than grass. Given the choice, cattle don't naturally eat grain. Rather, they'll roam around a paddock and eat anything green they can find. Unfortunately, it's a lot more economically efficient to keep cattle in pens and feed them bulk grains. They fatten more than on grass and they do it much more quickly.

A TALE OF TWO FATS

A diet high in grains does to beef cattle what it does to us: it increases the proportion of omega-6 fatty acids in the body fat. Grain-fed beef has an omega-6 to omega-3 ratio of 15:1 compared with the grass-fed ratio of about 2:1. Unlike us, cattle are ruminants and their gut removes any excess polyunsaturated fats, so the total polyunsaturated-fat content of their meat is the same whether they are grass-fed or grain-fed. But because the grains contain almost no omega-3 fats, the ratio is pushed out of kilter to the point that by the time they have been grain-fed for 56 days, half their omega-3 has been replaced with omega-6. After 112 days, they have just one-sixth of their starting omega-3, and after 196 days, all the omega-3 is gone.

Traditionally, beef production has been the process of converting grass into a product that humans will buy and eat. The best beef comes from fat cattle, which require good pasture. Until the 1970s, almost all Australian beef was entirely grass-fed. But that has changed rapidly over the last half-century.

Now, in Australia, all cattle still spend their early lives on pasture. They start on their mother's milk, and are weaned from pasture-based breeding cows between four and nine months of age. At this point, they weigh around 200 kilograms. They are then 'backgrounded' on pasture until they are about 12–18 months old. Once they reach a weight of 300–350 kilograms, they are generally sold to either a grass- or grain-finisher (feedlot). The average amount of time cattle spend on a grain feedlot is between 60 and 120 days, which is the last 10–20 per cent of their lifespan. In that time, they can be expected to gain about a third of their slaughter weight. Grass-finishing to the same weight takes about 50 per cent longer, which is why it's a less popular option.

WHAT DOES THAT BEEF LABEL MEAN?

There are no labelling standards for unpackaged meat sold fresh at retail outlets in Australia. Packaged meat has the same labelling requirements as all other processed food. But you will frequently come across extra claims on meat. Here is a list of what they mean.

Grass-fed: The animal has lived on a diet of grass its entire life. In the US, meat cannot be labelled 'grass-fed' unless this requirement is met. In Australia, there is no enforceable rule; we just have to trust the bloke supplying the meat.

Grain-fed: The animal was finished on grain (about one-third of its finished body weight and much of its usable meat weight comes from grains).

Grass-finished: See 'grass-fed'. By definition, cattle finished on grass are grass-fed, since all cattle start on grass. This meaningless marketing term is often added to make the beef sound even more grass-fed, for example, 'grass-fed and grass-finished'.

Grain-finished: See 'grain-fed'.

Organic: In the US, this term is legally defined to mean the animal was raised without hormones or antibiotics and its feed was pesticide-free. It does not mean the animal was grass-fed. In Australia, the term means whatever the marketer wants it to mean.

Certified organic: In Australia, this means the organic status has undergone a verification process that is laid out in an Australian standard. It still doesn't necessarily mean that the cattle were grass-fed.

Pasture-raised: All cattle are raised on pasture for some part of their life. The term is meaningless, and unenforceable, in Australia and the US.

The colour of an animal's fat provides a visual clue as to what it was fed. Grain-fed beef has pure white fat but the fat of grass-fed beef has a yellow tint. This is because carotene (the stuff that makes carrots orange) in grass colours the fat. The better the pasture, the more yellow the fat.

Today, around 40 per cent of Australia's total beef supply and 80 per cent of all beef sold in the major supermarkets is grain-finished. Feed grains represent the single biggest cost in a kilo of beef, pork and chicken. The chances are that if you are buying beef in the local supermarket, it is probably grain-fed. This doesn't mean you won't encounter the odd unlabelled grass-fed steak in the meat cabinet, but it is safer to assume most are grain-fed.

The good news is that if you are avoiding seed oils, and the occasional grain-fed steak is the only significant source of omega-6 in your diet, you are unlikely to be doing yourself any real harm. You'll be consuming perhaps half a gram more omega-6 per 100 grams than if you ate grass-fed beef only.

If you do decide to stick to grass-fed beef, you'll find that it's not impossible or even outrageously expensive to do it. A quick Google search will usually give you details of local farmers supplying the increasing demand for grass-fed beef in your area. Unfortunately, this usually means buying your meat in lots of at least $100 and hanging out at 'pick-up' points every few weeks for your bulk delivery. The upside is that the chap selling you the beef probably knows what the cow's name was and can definitely vouch for its grass-fed status. If you're less adventurous or just less hungry, Aldi has started carrying a line of reasonably priced grass-fed beef products. It even includes mince and costs only a little more than the grain-fed options, which it also sells. Most butchers can supply grass-fed beef if you ask, but once again, assume it's grain-fed if it doesn't say otherwise. Being in a butcher's-shop window does not necessarily make it grass-fed.

The good news is that if you are avoiding seed oils, and the occasional grain-fed steak is the only significant source of omega-6 in your diet, you are unlikely to be doing yourself any real harm.

Lamb

Traditionally, Australian sheep have been allowed to roam free on pasture and lot-feeding has only happened in drought and usually only accounted for 5–10 per cent of the lamb meat produced in any given year. But increasingly, prime lamb producers are turning to the predictability of supply (and income) that lot-feeding gives them. Approximately 40 per cent of Australian lamb is now lot-fed. Most of these lambs are lot-fed for the last half (eight weeks) of their lives and the feed in Australia is generally a hay, wheat, barley and sorghum mix (or hay, corn and soy in the US). Just like cattle, the grain feeding will result in a slightly higher proportion of omega-6 oil in the fat but even lot-fed lamb in Australia is relatively low in total polyunsaturated fats (about 1 gram per 100 grams). So there should be nothing stopping you indulging a taste for the other red meat, and if you spot lamb claiming to be grass-fed and your budget can stretch to it, it is always a better option.

Bacon and pork

Although most intensively farmed pigs are raised on grain, this is quite unnecessary. They can forage on pasture for two-thirds of their daily feed requirements and get the rest from fruit, vegetables, dairy products and grains. In Australia, it is illegal to feed pigs swill (waste products from meat, including scraps from our meat-based meals) because of the potential for foot-and-mouth disease, but they are terrific garbage-disposal units for anything edible.

In reality, only about 5 per cent of Australian pork is produced in what most of us would regard as free-range conditions. If you want to buy pork from these producers, you need to look out for meat that is certified by 'Australian Certified Organic', 'Australian Pork Free Range' or 'Humane Choice'. Allowing pigs to forage and supplying them with non-grain-based food supplements is, of course, very expensive when compared to the alternative and is done by few farmers.

Most pig meat comes from animals farmed in the pig equivalent of feedlots. Only 4.7 per cent of Australian pigs are raised on farms with fewer than 100 pigs. More than half of our pork comes from farms with more than 3000 pigs and more than three-quarters from farms with more than 1000 animals. Most Australian pigs live on commercial pig rations. Unlike cattle, pigs are grain-fed for their entire life (after being weaned from a grain-fed mother). Because of this almost exclusively grain-based diet, Australian pig meat is often relatively high in polyunsaturated fats.

Full-fat bacon will put a fair dent in your daily polyunsaturated fat allowance. As you can see in the chart over the page, 100 grams of bacon (two good-sized full-fat middle rashers) has about four times the polyunsaturated-fat content of 100 grams of beef sausage (one and a half thin snags) or bacon that has been 75 per cent trimmed. If you throw in a couple of eggs (1.4 grams each), you'll really be pushing it, with a total of 5.1 grams. This doesn't mean that bacon and eggs are off the menu, but if you plan to make it a daily treat then I'd suggest using trimmed bacon instead of full-fat, or sourcing a supply of bacon that has not been grain-fed. Vegetarian sausages are not a great option either because of the high soy content, so if you don't eat meat, mushrooms might be a better choice.

Eggs and chicken

Chickens normally eat grain so you might suspect that when you eat chicken and eggs, you are eating the products of an animal adapted to deal with high amounts of polyunsaturated fats. And while that is true, exactly which grains the chicken has been eating makes a big difference to the fats that end up in its meat or eggs. Meat and eggs from chickens fed an American commercial mix of corn and soybean meal have twice the concentrations of omega-6 fats as products from chickens fed a more typical Australian mixture of barley, wheat and sorghum meal.

Polyunsaturated-fat content of a range of popular meat and meat-substitute products

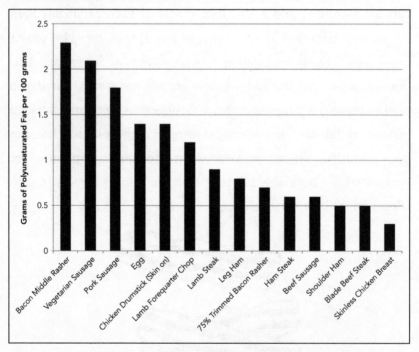

Source: Food Standards Australia NUTTAB 2010 (all meat cuts are untrimmed unless stated otherwise)

In Australia, economics are, for once, on the side of good health. Wheat and sorghum are the most commonly used grains in Australian chook food and are often supplemented with some soybean meal and animal fats. The overall omega-6 content in this kind of mixture is very similar to bread. This means that you need not fear the egg section of the supermarket or hesitate while collecting chicken from the deli. It does not mean that eggs and chicken are totally free from polyunsaturated fats, but it does mean that at the levels most people are likely to be consuming them, they are not of any great concern. You would have to be eating more than four Australian eggs a day before you exceeded your daily allowance of 6 grams of polyunsaturated fats. And, into the bargain, eggs contain a range of highly beneficial nutrients that few foods can match.

Milk

Just as with humans, the fats a cow consumes are transferred into her milk. The milk of grain-fed cows has much higher polyunsaturated-fat levels and a much higher omega-6 to omega-3 ratio than that of grass-fed cows. Fortunately, in Australia, feedlot dairies are relatively rare and most milk comes from grass-fed dairy cattle, but there are good economic reasons to change this, so don't be surprised if things don't stay that way. If you get a choice about where your meat and milk (and of course cheese, butter, cream and yoghurt) come from, choose grass-fed over grain-fed every time. But if it's not available at a price you can afford, don't panic. Just avoid the seed oils everywhere else in your diet and you'll be fine.

The milk of grain-fed cows has much higher polyunsaturated-fat levels and a much higher omega-6 to omega-3 ratio than that of grass-fed cows.

Non-dairy 'milk'

If you're already avoiding sugar then you're unlikely to be drinking soy, rice or almond milk, as almost all of these have added sugar. Diligent label readers will have discovered three fructose-free alternatives: Pure Harvest products are largely sweetened with rice malt syrup (essentially glucose), Vitasoy's Protein Enriched Rice Milk is not sweetened at all and Bonsoy is sweetened with tapioca syrup (also glucose). Bonsoy doesn't publish polyunsaturated fat content but based on total fat and ingredients it's likely to be very similar to Vitasoy Vanilla (1.1 grams per 100 ml). The bad news is that none of these products has a safe level of polyunsaturated fat when you remember that a glass of milk or a milk-based espresso coffee made with them will likely contain much more than 100 ml.

Almost all oat-, soy-, rice- and almond-based 'milks' are made with either sunflower or canola oil, sometimes both. An exception is Sanitarium's 99.9% Fat-Free soy. It contains the same low amount of polyunsaturated fat as cow's milk (0.1 gram per 100 ml). Unfortunately, it also contains one teaspoon of cane sugar in every cup (250 ml). If you're just adding a splash of soy milk to your tea or coffee, choose something with the lowest sugar content you can

find. If you plan to drink it by the glass or add it to your porridge in quantity, coconut milks with no added oil or sugar are the way to go, such as So Good Unsweetened Coconut Milk.

If you're avoiding cow's milk because of lactose intolerance and don't like coconuts, one of the enzyme-treated milks such as Pauls Zymil is the best option. It is ordinary cow's milk treated with the lactase enzyme that lactose-intolerant people are missing, which disassembles lactose into its components, galactose and glucose, and should present no problems for lactose tolerance.

Baby formula

If you have an infant hanging around the place, you don't have a lot of choices about how to feed her. Her mother's milk is obviously the best choice, but not always possible, and in that case, you're left with commercial formula.

Babies are in the business of growing stuff, and during the critical early-growth stages, infants are building their brains, immune systems, nervous systems and eyes, all of which require omega-6 and omega-3 polyunsaturated fats. Since we can't make these fats, mothers need to be very good at extracting them from their food and transferring them to the baby via their milk. It appears that there is no control mechanism for extracting these polyunsaturated fats. We seem to be built on the assumption that these fats are scarce and that we will give as much as we can get to the baby. Women pass up to 75 per cent of consumed polyunsaturated fat directly into breast milk. That's no big deal when the mother's diet is low in polyunsaturated fats, but if her diet is dominated by omega-6 fats, the baby will be receiving a significant dose of something for which she has no evolutionary precedent.

Studies on various populations clearly illustrate this huge variation. Bedouin women eating a largely meat-based diet will produce breast milk in which 6 per cent of the fat is polyunsaturated. Women consuming lard as their only source of fat will have milk fat that is 10 per cent polyunsaturated, and the milk fat of women on a Lebanese or Mediterranean diet (where fat is 70 per cent animal fat and 30 per cent olive oil) will be 11 per cent polyunsaturated. But women provided with polyunsaturated seed oil (corn oil) as their only source of fat will produce milk that is 42 per cent polyunsaturated.

A breastfeeding woman consuming all or most of her fats from seed oils – a situation that's increasingly difficult to avoid – will be quadrupling her baby's omega-6 consumption.

Polyunsaturated fat content of cow's milk, human milk and popular commercial baby formulas (that publish breakdowns)

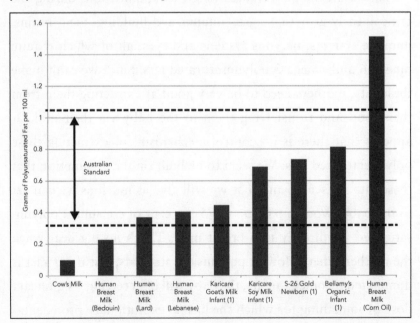

An Australian mother eating a diet largely devoid of seed oils will be supplying breast milk containing about 0.33 grams of omega-6 fats and 0.04 grams of omega-3 fats for every 100 ml of milk. These amounts are in line with averages from well-fed societies the world over, and are the perfect amounts required by a growing baby. If instead she feeds the baby using Bellamy's Organic Infant formula, for example, she'll be doubling those quantities.

Babies need omega-6 and omega-3 fats, which are critical to the development of fully functional eyesight and early components of both the brain and nervous system. We grow our brains in the first two years of life – our brains triple in size during that time. And these polyunsaturated fats, and the longer versions we use these to construct, make up about 20 per cent of our brain's final dry weight. If a mother is eating a diet that results in her supplying less than 3 per cent of her milk fats as omega-6 fats, which is virtually impossible unless she is severely malnourished, then the infant will have delayed growth, poor wound healing and skin lesions, and is likely to suffer long-term developmental problems. But omega-6 and omega-3 fatty acids compete for the same metabolic pathways and enzymes. Flooding an infant's system with excess omega-6 results in the metabolism and use of omega-3 fats being blocked. There are no studies suggesting there is any benefit whatsoever in providing more omega-6 fats to infants than the amounts which appear in the breast milk of a mother eating a wholefood diet without seed oils, around 8.5 per cent of total fats, while the Australian standard for formula is a minimum of 9 per cent. There are many concerns now being raised about developmental disorders associated with the displacement of omega-3 fats with omega-6.

There are many concerns now being raised about developmental disorders associated with the displacement of omega-3 fats with omega-6.

The best way to minimise the potential to overconsume these fats is to breastfeed while avoiding seed oils. If that is not possible, the next best option available in an Australian supermarket today is Karicare's Goat's Milk formula.

Once the baby moves on to solids, commercial cereals such as Farex should also be avoided as they all contain added seed oils.

How to read a label

The previous section is not a complete listing of every food you will encounter – that would be impossible (and boring). When you're flying solo through a new-product category, here are some rules I have found handy.

There's an old mafia saying: 'The best place to hide a body is in a massacre.' Food labels work on the same principle. They throw numbers, columns and unrecognisable words at us in the hope that we don't find the 'body' – the dangerous stuff we need to know about. Most of what you need to know is right there on the label, it's just buried in a thousand things you don't to know. But don't worry, here's a crash course in what matters and what doesn't on a food label. Our test subject today is 'Praise Whole Egg Mayonnaise with Olive Oil'.

The front label suggests this might be a food we could eat. It has a picture of an olive and an egg and doesn't say anything to suggest there are any ingredients of concern. In fact, it looks like it might be a bit of a find, since every other commercial mayo sold in Australia is made with seed oil (mostly sunflower oil). So, let's look at the detail.

Here's the nutritional information:

	Per Serving (20 g)	%DI* Per Serving (20 g)	Per 100 g
Energy (kj)	510	6	2530
Protein (g)	less than 1	1	1.7
Gluten	0	0	0
Fats (g)	13.3	19	66.3
Saturated Fat (g)	1.8	8	9
Carbohydrate (g)	less than 1	less than 1	2.6
Sugars (g)	less than 1	1	2.4
Sodium (mg)	115	5	565

Step 1

Ignore the 'Per serving' and '%DI' (percentage of the average adult male's recommended daily intake) columns.

Step 2

Examine the grams of sugar per 100 grams. As the product has less than my recommended rule of thumb (3 grams per 100 grams), it's fine.

Step 3

Polyunsaturated fat doesn't have to be labelled in Australia, so we need to do a bit of detective work to figure out what might be there. Look at how much 'Saturated fat' there is compared to 'Fat'. In this case, the fraction of saturated fat is 9/66, which is about 13.5 per cent. Anything less than 30 per cent is probably not an animal fat, palm oil or coconut oil. Thirteen per cent could be olive oil or it could be a seed oil, so let's keep looking.

Step 4

Look at the ingredients list below. Ingredients are listed in descending order of weight. So, the ingredient that's the biggest component of the product is listed first and then the next and so on. In this case, the primary ingredient is sunflower oil, a seed oil. The next ingredient is water and then egg. Then comes olive oil, but it's just 8.75 per cent of the product. If an ingredient is mentioned on the front of the pack, the manufacturer must state how much of that ingredient the product contains – this is why there's no percentage after sunflower oil, but there is one after the egg and the olive oil.

Ingredients

Sunflower oil [antioxidant (320)], water, free range whole egg (10.5%), olive oil (8.75%), white vinegar, Dijon mustard [food acid (260)], sugar, whey protein concentrate (milk), lemon juice concentrate [food acid (330)], salt, vegetable gums (405, 415), garlic.

After we do a little label-reading, the initially promising product turns out to be just another seed-oil mayo. You might be thinking we could have just skipped to Step 4, but this is an unusually honest product. Many will not identify the oil, and simply say 'vegetable oil'. But since we'd have ruled out animal fat, palm oil and coconut oil (in Step 3) and they'd very likely say if olive oil was an ingredient (because it's expensive), in that case it would be safe to assume that the 'vegetable oil' meant a seed oil.

As a general guide, seed oils are used to make baked food crispy and sauces gooey. Mixer sauces (the sort of pre-made sauce that turns your chicken or mince into something flash) often include vegetable oils and should be avoided, even if you aren't worried about their sugar content. And, of course, you'll also find vegetable oils in many breakfast cereals for that crunch-in-the-mouth feel, except raw oat- and wheat-based

As a general guide, seed oils are used to make baked food crispy and sauces gooey.

products. Bizarrely, you'll also find vegetable oils in liquid versions of breakfast cereals, such as Sanitarium's 'Up & Go' range. Almost everything in the freezer section (except for plain, snap-frozen vegetables) will contain seed oils or sugar or both.

If the food you are considering is neither crunchy nor saucy (nor any of the items I've discussed above – spreads, breads, fried food and so on), you're likely to be on to a winner, but check the label to be sure.

Eating out

If you purchase anything to eat, almost all the fat components will be seed oils. The mayo on your takeaway sandwich will be made from sunflower oil, as will the margarine. Anything fried will have been cooked in cottonseed or canola oil, no matter how flash the joint you purchased it from. All the breads and other baked goods will have been made using seed oils and so will all the dressings, dips and sauces.

Fried food

Takeaway deep-fried food contains large quantities of oil, and it's now almost impossible to buy a deep-fried food in Australia cooked in anything other than seed oil. The big-brand fast-food joints (such as McDonald's and KFC) use canola–sunflower blends, but even the

Seed oils do not contain cholesterol. They don't contain asbestos either but that doesn't make them healthy.

corner fish and chipper is likely to be using 'vegetable oil'. In the flash outlets, that usually means cottonseed or canola oil; in the not-so-flash, it's likely to be blended vegetable oils, usually a blend of cottonseed, canola and sunflower oil. A dead giveaway is a proudly displayed sign saying something like: 'Our food is fried in cholesterol-free oil.' Seed oils do not contain cholesterol. They don't contain asbestos either but that doesn't make them healthy.

My local fish 'n' chip joint doesn't publish the fat content of its foods, but McDonald's does. Before the intervention of the Australian Heart Foundation, Maccas fries contained barely any seed oil and so barely any polyunsaturated fats. A large serving would have you consuming just under 1 gram of the stuff. But now, that same serve of fries will deliver more than five times as much of the fat that is the very worst for your health. You'll almost blow your daily allowance of polyunsaturated fat with just one large serving of Maccas fries.

It's a lot more than fries that get dunked in the fat at McDonalds. Here's a list of the foods that contain at least one element that is deep-fried and therefore high in polyunsaturated fat:

- McChicken (burger)
- Chicken 'n' Cheese (burger)
- Crispy Chicken (salads, burgers and wraps)
- Filet-O-Fish (burger)
- Chicken McNuggets
- Fries
- Hash Brown
- Apple Pie

McDonald's fries – then and now

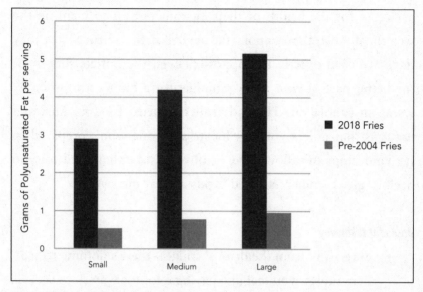

Source: McDonald's Australia (based on 2018 serving sizes)

It's not just the fried foods that contain seed oil, either. Almost all the condiments, any product that contains bread and most of the cakes and other desserts at McCafé also contain seed oils. The amount of seed oil used in most of these products is quite small, but I've mentioned them to give you a feel for how pervasive seed oils have become in our food supply. I'm using McDonald's as an example because they are one of the few fast-food joints that publish detailed ingredient lists of everything they sell. It is reasonably safe to assume that similar ingredients are being used at Hungry Jack's and every other place purveying chips and burgers, and probably even those selling cakes and coffee. Until recently, KFC had been a viable alternative from a nutritional perspective, but in May 2012, even they announced that they were switching from Malaysian palm oil to Australian-grown canola oil. They trumpeted the change as a victory for the health of their customers (not to mention the wealth of Australian canola farmers) but the science says they have achieved exactly the opposite. Even the outlets that want the better part of your weekly budget for a burger are probably frying in canola oil. The sad reality of fried food in Australia today is that unless you can locate someone who's prepared to fry your chips in tallow, lard or olive oil like they used to, you need to give commercial fried foods a great big swerve.

Rules for takeaway

- Stay away from the drinks' fridge – there's nothing to see here (unless you feel like paying a lot for water).
- Don't order anything deep-fried unless you know the establishment is using olive oil or animal fat (extremely unlikely, so don't assume it).
- Don't even think about the ice-cream fridge.
- Don't buy sauces to go with the meal and, if the sauce usually comes on board (such as with a hamburger), ask for your meal to be made without it.
- Avoid any kind of sandwich spread unless you know it is butter, and don't buy anything with mayo.

Pizza

Depending how much of it you eat, pizza is a fairly low-sugar and low-seed-oil option. The sauce is the primary source of sugar, and the base is the primary source of seed oil. Because 'meat lover's' pizzas use barbecue sauce, they tend to be the highest-sugar pizzas. Hawaiian pizzas include pineapple and, depending on how much they put on, this can push their sugar rating up. Pepperoni pizzas are generally the lowest-sugar option because they are just meat and a straight tomato sauce. These numbers apply equally across most takeaway outlets. All chain pizza joints use seed oils in their bases but, unless you're planning to eat a whole large pizza yourself (something you will probably find physically impossible once you quit sugar), the amount of seed oil you will be consuming is not so significant that you need to worry about it (see next page for detailed calculations).

The thickness of the pizza base makes a big difference to the amount of seed oil you'll be consuming. If you prefer pan base, the amount of oil will increase by approximately 25 per cent. If you prefer thin, it will decrease by the same amount. If you're avoiding polyunsaturated fats but you don't want to give up takeaway pizza, choose a thin base and limit yourself to three slices. This way, you'll probably only consume about 1.1 grams of polyunsaturated fat. If you're trying to decide whether to have Pizza Hut or Maccas for dinner, the pizza is definitely a better choice (unless you weren't planning to have anything fried with your burger, in which case they'd be about the same).

A standard takeaway piece of pizza weighs about 80 grams, so one piece of meat lover's or Hawaiian could give you up to one teaspoon of sugar. A reasonable rule of thumb is that there is half a teaspoon of sugar in every slice of pizza you buy, so if you eat three slices, you'll be having a teaspoon and a half of sugar with your 1.1 grams of polyunsaturated fat. Neither will kill you but neither is ideal either, so it's probably best to have bought pizza as an occasional treat only. Garlic breads vary between nothing and around 3 per cent sugar, and are often based on a bread made with canola oil (usually about 1 gram per 100 grams), so adding this to your order increases both the sugar and the oil count. There is also no guarantee that they use real butter. If you can live without it, do.

Asian foods

Most of us encounter Asian foods at our local corner restaurant. The food is usually cooked according to the whim of the owner and the nutrition content is not measured or published. This makes it almost impossible to provide guidance on what to eat in the same way that I have elsewhere, but I'll give it a go.

Brown sugar or palm sugar is often a primary ingredient in Thai and Chinese sauces and an important component in others, and seed oils are a primary ingredient in commercial curry pastes. Since sauces and pastes tend to be the essence of much Asian food, this can be a problem. If you're eating out, these guidelines will help.

Rules for eating out Asian-style
- When possible, stick to Chinese or Indian cuisine rather than going for Thai or Malaysian.

- Stay away from anything that mentions honey or sweet chilli.
- Avoid anything that says it contains, or was fried in, peanut oil or sesame oil.
- Don't eat the prawn crackers or any other fried part of the dish unless you know what it was fried in – and that it wasn't any kind of seed oil.

You don't have to go cold turkey on Asian food; you just have to know that it is dangerous territory and that you are risking significant exposure to sugar and seed oils if you eat out and don't know how the food is being cooked. It is possible (and easy) to make most Asian dishes from scratch using ingredients that contain no or minimal sugar and seed oil. Give it a go – it's fun and, with the money you save, you could take yourself on an Asian holiday instead.

If you are assembling your own Asian foods, you'll be using pastes and sauces to provide the flavour to a base of meat or fish, vegetables and carbohydrates, usually noodles or rice. Rice is a fine choice as a meal base because it has neither added seed oil nor added sugar. Most noodles are fine too, as long as you avoid the 'instant' noodles, which are often pre-fried in seed oil (check the ingredients list – no oil should be listed). If you are using a kit, such as Marion's Kitchen, you will see that you are advised to add vegetable oil during the assembly process. Simply change that to olive oil and you'll be fine from a seed-oil perspective but pay careful attention to the sugar content. If you are cooking at home, be selective about which brand of sauce and paste you use because the sugar content varies significantly between brands.

For example, Chang's Hoisin (7.1 per cent) has less than a fifth of Woolworths Hoisin (45 per cent).

The good news is that most Asian sauces, except for sesame seed oil, contain no appreciable amount of polyunsaturated fat. Unfortunately, sesame seed oil is 44 per cent polyunsaturated fat and should be avoided for anything other than flavouring with very small quantities. In place of sesame oil, you can use any of the 'safe' fats and oils I set out in the table on page 30, but you will miss out on that sesame-seed taste. The best way to simulate it is to use a cooking oil that doesn't have much flavour (such as light olive oil) and throw in some whole sesame seeds for flavour.

If you're a curry fiend, you will need to be disciplined enough to steer well clear of the curry-paste supermarket shelf. Almost every brand of pre-made curry paste has sunflower or soybean oil as a primary ingredient. The only real option is to invest in a good spice rack and a mortar and pestle. You'll find thousands of recipes for your favourite curry within seconds on Google, or if you prefer a recipe book, Christine Manfield and Kylie Kwong both have great recipes for DIY pastes. Just remember to leave out the sugar and substitute olive oil (or macadamia oil, if you're feeling wealthy) whenever you are told to add vegetable oil.

Mexican food

I have good news and bad news for Mexican food lovers. The good news is that aside from the wrapping (taco shells or tortillas), Mexican food rarely contains added seed oil. The bad news is that it is often seasoned with sauces that are a sugar minefield.

If you like your Mexican food wrapped in a tortilla or burrito, most brands use palm oil (appearing as 'vegetable oil' on the label) and add very little sugar but check the label first. As long as the seasoning and salsa you are using contains less than 3 grams of sugar per 100 grams, you won't be getting much more sugar from the filling either.

If you prefer taco shells, the best choice is the Old El Paso brand. They have half the polyunsaturated fat of the others because they are made using the modified sunflower oil used to make crisps and corn chips rather than standard sunflower or canola oil. But I wouldn't worry too much; 100 grams of taco shells is nine standard or five jumbo tacos, so unless you really pig out, you won't be doing a whole lot of damage to your daily allowance of omega-6 fats.

Shopping directory

There are some processed foods you can get away with buying. Sure, it's better to make everything from scratch, but increasingly some manufacturers are paying attention to our desire to have basic real food devoid of sugar and seed oils. The following lists contain food that's either completely free of added sugar and seed oil, or an acceptable compromise. I've laid out the best choices in each category and also listed those you can use with caution.

Raw fats
- Olive oil
- Coconut oil
- Avocado oil
- Sustainable palm oil and palm kernel oil
- High oleic sunflower oil

- Macadamia oil
- Chestnut oil
- Butter
- Ghee
- Animal fat (including Supafry lard, tallow, fowl fat, etc.)

Seeds and nuts

- All whole, unprocessed legumes
- Any whole nuts but go for chestnuts, coconut, macadamias, hazelnuts, cashews and pistachios

Use with Caution:

- Avoid seeds unless used as a garnish or flavouring
- Whole almonds (really a seed) or peanuts

Breads

- Sourdoughs
- European-style breads (but check ingredients)
- Aldi's Pane di Casa white loaf
- Burgen Rye (best non-white bread)

Use with Caution:

- Coles White and Bakery White
- Woolworths White, Wholemeal and Country Loaf White
- Tip Top® Sunblest® White, Wholemeal and Multigrain

Wraps and tacos

- Mountain Bread wraps
- Old El Paso taco shells

Flour

- Potato
- White rice
- Wheat
- Rye (light)
- Barley

Spreads, condiments, snacks, etc.

- Butter
- Mainland Buttersoft
- Vegemite
- Avocado
- Unflavoured cream cheese
- Sanitarium Peanut Butter
- Good Fat Mayo from Undivided Food Co.
- Greenland sundried tomatoes
- Chang's Hoisin

Dressings

- Praise Italian 100% Fat Free

Use with Caution:

- Paul Newman's Own Light Balsamic Vinaigrette and Classic Balsamic Vinaigrette
- Praise Fat-Free Balsamic, Balsamic, French, Greek and Italian
- Coles Caesar
- Birch & Waite Balsamic, Greek-Style and Caesar

Biscuits

- Arnott's Rice, Rye and Corn Cruskits
- Arnott's Salada 97% Fat-free Multigrain, Wholemeal and Light Original
- San-J Tamari Brown Rice Crackers

Chips

- Red Rock Deli Salted Potato Chips
- Woolworths Deli Style

Use with Caution:

- Any other brand of plain salted crisps or plain corn chips

Frozen goods

- McCain Healthy Choice Straight Cut Chips
- Coles Straight Cut Chips
- McCain Superfries Steak Cut and Steak Cut Chips
- McCain frozen pizza base
- Naturally Gluten Free pizza base
- All other frozen vegetables

Use with Caution:

- All other brands of frozen chips

Fish

- Bream, oysters, tuna, cod, scallop, flathead, lobster, prawns and calamari (squid)
- Salmon if you know it's sustainably wild-caught or farmed by Tassal in Tasmania

- Tinned fish, but only tinned in water
- If you must eat caviar, choose red over black

Use with Caution:

- Any other fresh fish

Meat and meat products

- Poultry and eggs
- Grass-fed meat

Use with Caution:

- Grain-fed meat, but don't worry too much about this especially for beef
- Sausages, rissoles, crumbed fillets and other pre-made meat and poultry products are usually fine, but check the ingredients list. If it includes sugar or 'vegetable oil', avoid it. Be especially careful of crumbed products – soy flour is usually an ingredient, as is vegetable oil.

Dairy (and imitation dairy)

- Whole fat or low-fat milk
- So Good Unsweetened Coconut Milk
- Pauls Zymil (lactose-free milk)
- Cream
- Cheese
- Unsweetened yoghurt

Use with Caution:

- Sanitarium's So Good 99.9% Fat-Free
- Coles Lite Soy Milk

- So Natural Rice Milk
- Vitasoy Lite
- Sanitarium Lite

Pastry

- Carème Butter Puff Pastry
- Pampas Butter Puff Pastry

3
Recipes

I've mentioned every now and then that it is impossible to easily buy a given type of food and be sure it contains no seed oil. Most takeaway fried food is cooked in seed oil. All mayonnaise sold in our local supermarket is based on seed oil, as are almost all the dips and pesto.

As our family has stumbled through the task of ridding our lives of seed oils, we've occasionally decided we really don't want to live without a certain food (hot chips spring immediately to mind). And so we have set about reconstructing that food without seed oil. Often that has involved finding a recipe that used seed oil and tweaking it so that olive oil can be used instead. Sometimes it has simply involved finding out where to get a seed-oil-free ingredient. The results of our labours appear in the recipes that follow. You don't need to be a chef. All the recipes are simple, quick enough to make on a daily basis if you want to, and – best of all – completely free of seed oil and fructose.

The sweet recipes use the glucose half of sugar as the sweetener. In essence, it's sugar without the dangerous bit (fructose). It's available in three common forms: dextrose, which is powdered glucose that looks like caster sugar but is nowhere near as sweet; glucose syrup; and rice malt syrup, which looks and tastes like honey but is also nowhere near as sweet. All three are treated like pure glucose by our bodies.

Dextrose and rice malt syrup are available in supermarkets but supply can be unreliable. We have found that some Big W stores (and sometimes Woolworths) stock dextrose in the home-brewing section (next to the energy drinks). Be careful not to buy brewing sugar or maltodextrin – they're not the same thing. Coles usually stocks rice malt syrup in the health-food section or sometimes in the cooking section. If they don't have it, they'll have 'glucose syrup' in the cooking section. It can be substituted for rice malt syrup – you'll just lose the slightly malty flavour. If your local supermarket doesn't carry these, ask. Many will get them in if they know there are customers wanting it.

A very good online supplier is The Sugar Breakup (shop. thesugarbreakup.com), an Australian company that caters for people avoiding fructose. Dextrose can also be bought from anyone selling home-brewing supplies (for example Dan Murphy's and Brigalow), while rice malt syrup is available from online health-food stores. Many of the following sweet recipes originally appeared in the *Eat Real Food Cookbook* or *Sweet Poison Quit Plan Cookbook* but, as some people prefer not to use animal fat, we've recreated them here using olive oil instead of butter.

Bread

When Lizzie first began making bread, the recipe involved lots of kneading and proving, and was much too time-consuming to do on a daily basis, especially with teenage boys in the family, who eat more bread than anyone without teenage boys can imagine. She tried many different variations on the art of bread construction but eventually came back to where she started with this simple set of recipes.

Yeast bread

This versatile recipe, which first appeared as pizza dough in *Toxic Oil*, is perfect not only for bread, but also for pizza bases, cheese and bacon rolls and, of course, breadcrumbs. If your favourite bread is supermarket white, this loaf might take some getting used to. It's similar when fresh, but crumblier and less springy when a little older. It's still great for toast and, best of all, it contains no added seed oils or sugar. Using semolina in the last knead gives a crisper crust, but you can easily omit it.

600 g plain flour, plus extra for
dusting
2 generous teaspoons
dried yeast
1 teaspoon salt

1½ cups lukewarm water
¼ cup extra virgin olive oil
2 tablespoons semolina
(optional)

1. Preheat oven to 200°C. Grease and flour a 21 cm × 10 cm loaf tin.
2. Combine flour, yeast and salt in a bowl, and make a well in the centre.

3. Pour the warm water and olive oil into the well then mix until a dough forms. This is quite a wet mixture, so it may help to knead it in the bowl until it's less sticky.

4. Transfer the dough to a smooth, clean, dry surface and form it into a ball. Using the heel of your hand, push the centre of the dough ball down and away from you. Bring the far edge of the dough up and back towards you, then press it into the middle of the ball again. Repeat this kneading step until the dough is soft and smooth (about 8–10 minutes). Alternatively, you could use the dough hook on an electric mixer. When the dough is ready it will be smooth and will bounce back from a nudge with your finger.

5. Place the dough ball in a bowl greased with butter or olive oil, cover with cling wrap or a plate and leave in a warm place for 1 hour to prove; it should double in size.

6. Sprinkle with a little flour or the semolina (if you have it) mixed with some flour on your board or benchtop. Knead the dough on this lightly floured surface until smooth.

7. Shape into a loaf, slash three diagonal grooves across the top and gently transfer to the tin.

8. Leave the tin in a warm, draught-free spot (such as above the oven) for 30 minutes or until the loaf has doubled in size.

9. Bake for about 30 minutes or until the loaf is crusty and sounds hollow when tapped on the bottom. The loaf may rise further during cooking, so make sure there is no shelf too close above it. (Optional: at about the 20-minute mark, spritz the loaf with a little water while in the oven to give the crust a bit of a glaze.)

10. Turn the loaf out of the tin and cool on a wire rack.

Sourdough bread

This brilliantly easy recipe first appeared in *Toxic Oil*. Most sourdough you pick up in the shops will be sugar-free, but if you buy it from a supermarket it's likely to have been made with canola oil. Once you have your sourdough starter up and running, it will take you less than 5 minutes each day to prepare a loaf and you'll never need to do any kneading (or any other messing about). If you don't want to get up early to get your bread cooking, mix the ingredients before work, leave the mix to stand all day and cook it in the evening. It will still be delicious the next morning.

The starter

Don't be put off by the number of steps – they're all simple and you only need to do them once. The trick to this recipe is the 'starter' – a living culture that you feed with flour every few days. Our sourdough starter has been going strong for the past four years. We even take it on holidays with us! There it sits, in its little jar in the corner of the fridge, brewing up the foundation for tomorrow's bread. Once your starter is established, all you need to do is replace what you take out to make bread with some flour and water if you're baking a loaf every other day. If you're only baking once or twice a week, you'll need to remove and replenish the water and flour as if you were still baking regularly.

The only really important thing to know is that your starter mustn't be contaminated with any commercial yeasts or they will take over. Always use a clean spoon to deal with your starter (removing, replenishing and mixing). You might need to add some dried yeast to your first few loaves of bread dough (but not the starter) because there won't yet be enough bacteria in the starter to make the dough rise. Once the starter is going strong, though, all you'll need is some flour, salt, water and time for it to make you a perfect loaf every time. Once the starter is established, leave it in the fridge and feed it when you use it to make bread.

Day 1

Find a home for your new pet starter. A jar is ideal – it needs to protect the contents without being completely airtight. We use a large old glass Moccona coffee jar (with the pop-top plastic-based lid). In the jar, mix together 50 g plain flour, 50 ml water and 2 tablespoons Greek yoghurt. Loosely put the lid on the jar and leave in a warm but not hot place overnight.

Day 2

Using a clean spoon (always – any contamination with yeast will destroy it), add 100 g flour and 100 ml water. Stir to combine (it's easiest to mix in both the water and flour at the same time), re-cover and return to its warm spot.

Day 3

This is your first day of actual bread-making, if you choose. Today you will be taking some starter out and putting new 100 g flour and 100 ml water in. Remove 200 g from your starter to make your first loaf (see method on page 99). The young starter will give your loaf a sourdough flavour, but it's still just a baby pet, so you'll need to add yeast to your bread mixture. If you want to wait until you can make bread without yeast, just discard the 200 g. Whichever you choose, feed your pet (once again with a clean spoon) with 100 g flour and 100 ml water. Stir them in, put the lid back on and put it back in its warm spot.

Day 4

From now on, repeat the removal of 200 g starter every day – either discarding it or baking with it (still with yeast at this stage), then replenishing with 100 g flour and 100 ml water, mixing, covering and returning to its warm spot.

Days 10–15

At some point, your starter will become quite a bit more active (and it could take a week or more – longer in colder climates and/or winter, so be patient). It will bubble and froth in the bottle and, due to that aeration, will appear to almost double in size between refills. Once this has occurred, your starter is established. From now on you can keep it in the fridge (to stop it growing too quickly and/or spilling out of the jar) and use it to bake sourdough without any yeast. 'Feed' your starter twice a week (using a clean spoon to take out 200 g and replacing with 100 g flour and 100 ml water), or as often as you bake. Don't worry if it looks like there's not much starter left after you take 200 g out – an established starter can bounce back from just a very small sample. Even just a dirty jar will be enough.

The sourdough loaf

200 g sourdough starter
(see page 97)
375 g plain flour,
plus extra for dusting
275 ml water

1 teaspoon fine-grained salt
(optional)
¼ teaspoon dried yeast (if
starter not yet established)

1. In a large bowl, combine the starter, flour, water and salt (and yeast if your starter is still young).

2. Cover with cling wrap and leave in a warm place for at least 8 hours but 12 hours if possible.

3. Preheat the oven to 200°C and grease and flour a 21 cm × 10 cm loaf tin or a round cast-iron pot. (A non-stick tin won't need flouring and a silicone mould won't either.)

4. Using a plastic or silicone spatula (the sticky and elastic mixture is impossible to manipulate with anything else), manoeuvre the mixture into the tin. Sit the tin on a metal baking tray. We use the metal tray to easily remove the silicone mould from the oven (because they are floppy).

5. Bake for 45 minutes or until the loaf is crusty on top and sounds hollow when tapped on the bottom. If you like it really crusty leave it in for another 15–20 minutes.

6. Turn the loaf out of the tin and cool on a wire rack for about 30 minutes before tucking in. It's great fresh but it's better toasted after a day or so.

No-knead bread

If sourdough is not your thing or you don't want to mess around with growing and feeding a starter, then this is the bread for you. The method is exactly the same as for the sourdough loaf, but you compensate for not having the starter by using extra flour and water.

425 g plain flour

1½ cups water

1 teaspoon fine-grained salt

¼ teaspoon dried yeast

Use the same method as for the sourdough loaf.

No-knead refrigerator bread

Lizzie's friend Beth alerted her to this extraordinarily quick and easy recipe for producing bread with almost no effort. It combines the ease of not having to knead with not needing to even plan ahead. This version is adapted from one at www.jezebel.com.

3 cups lukewarm water

1½ tablespoons salt

1½ tablespoons dried yeast

975 g plain flour

1. Take one large container with a sealable lid. This is your mixing bowl and storage container.
2. Put the water and the salt in the container, then add in the yeast and stir. Let the mixture sit until it starts bubbling (a few minutes).
3. Add the flour and stir until you have sticky dough with no lumps of dry flour.
4. Put the lid on loosely and leave the container on the bench until the dough rises to the top (this could take a couple of hours).
5. Punch it down enough to get the lid on, then seal the lid properly and put it in the fridge.
6. Leave it in the fridge for a few hours before your first use. The dough will last about 3 weeks in the fridge.
7. Whenever you want to make fresh homemade bread, grab a lump of the dough and throw it into a greased loaf tin, then into a 230°C preheated oven. If you prefer bread rolls then just roll the dough into little balls and place them on an oven tray at the same temperature.
8. 35 minutes later (20 for the bread rolls) you will have perfect home-baked bread with a golden crust.

You can do this every time you want bread until the dough is used then just refill the container (steps 1–5) and start all over again. You will never be more than half an hour away from fresh bread again.

Roti or chapatti bread

We used to have a nice pack of shop-bought deep-fried pappa-dums with our homemade chicken curry on a Monday night (you need a schedule when you're feeding six kids). When we discovered they were cooked in seed oil, we went looking for a substitute we could make ourselves that didn't involve getting out the deep-fryer just for a side dish. You could of course buy pre-made traditional pappadums and deep-fry them in animal fat instead of the suggested seed oil, but this really simple recipe produces a delicious seed-oil-free chapatti bread in just minutes. (And if you like, you can even use it as a yeast-free pizza base.) If you want a nuttier flavour, use half wholemeal flour.

Makes 8

225 g plain flour
   (plus extra for dusting)
¼ teaspoon salt

1 cup water
olive oil or butter for frying

1. In a bowl, mix together flour and salt.
2. Make a well in the centre and gradually add in the water until the mixture forms a supple dough.
3. Knead on a lightly floured surface until smooth (up to 7 minutes), then allow dough to sit for 15–20 minutes if you have time (we rarely have time, and the recipe still works).
4. Divide dough into 8 portions and, on a floured surface, roll each into a thin round.
5. Place a frying pan over high heat. Once heated, lower the temperature to medium, brush with oil or butter and place

a chapatti in the pan. Once bubbles appear on the surface, flip the chapatti and cook briefly until coloured but not yet crisp.

6. Remove chapatti from the frying pan and keep warm while you cook more, then serve with curry.

Pizza dough

These seed-oil-free, sugar-free pizza bases taste great and also freeze very well (with or without topping), so you can make a big batch and fill the freezer for quick and easy meals in the future.

Makes 6 medium or 3 large thin bases

2 teaspoons dried yeast

600 g plain flour

1 teaspoon salt

1½ cups warm water

¼ cup olive oil, plus extra for brushing

1. In a large bowl, combine all dry ingredients.
2. Place wet ingredients together in a jug.
3. Make a well in the centre of the dry ingredients, and pour in the wet ingredients.
4. Bring mixture together with your hands.
5. Turn mixture onto a floured surface and knead for up to 10 minutes (or use the dough hook on the mixer), until a smooth, elastic dough forms.
6. Place dough in a lightly oiled bowl, cover, and rest (the dough, not you) in a warm spot for 30 minutes, if there is time.
7. Preheat oven to 210°C.
8. Divide dough evenly into the number of pizzas you plan to make.
9. Roll out and add whatever toppings you like before shoving pizzas into the preheated oven for 15 minutes or until they look cooked.

Hamburger buns

If you're making hamburgers at home and want to completely avoid seed oils and sugar, you won't be able to use supermarket buns. If money is no object, you could use most European-style bread rolls from the bakery. But if you want to have some fun, try this recipe.

When we first made these, we couldn't believe how good they were. Since then, the only time they haven't worked was when I left the milk heating too long and, being impatient, didn't let it cool to a tepid temperature. That killed the yeast and made the rolls a bit flatter and smaller than usual, though still tasty enough to be eaten! If hot dogs are your thing, this recipe works just as well with different-shaped bread rolls.

This recipe becomes exceedingly easy if you have an electric mixer with a dough hook. If not, roll up your sleeves and you won't knead to go to the gym today . . .

Makes 12 buns

1 cup milk	3 teaspoons dried yeast
½ cup water	1½ teaspoons salt
60 g butter	2 eggs – 1 lightly beaten, and
750 g plain flour, plus extra for flouring surface	1 (optional) for basting

1. Preheat oven to 200°C.
2. Warm milk, water and butter together until tepid (too hot and it will kill the yeast, too cold and the yeast won't activate).
3. In a separate bowl, mix flour, yeast and salt.
4. Add one lightly beaten egg to the dry ingredients, followed gradually by the milk mixture until a dough forms.

5. Mix in an electric mixer with a dough hook for 10 minutes or knead for same amount of time on a floured surface until smooth and elastic.

6. Divide dough into 12 equal pieces, shaping each into a smooth ball.

7. Place the balls onto lined baking trays (leaving gaps between them for the buns to rise), flatten slightly, cover with a clean tea towel and leave to rest for 30 minutes in a warm place.

8. If basting, beat second egg in a bowl and brush top of buns gently with a small amount of egg.

9. Bake in preheated oven for 10–12 minutes until golden-brown.

10. Remove from oven and cool on a wire rack before using.

Plain damper

Makes 1 loaf or 8 rolls

450 g plain flour

pinch of salt

2 teaspoons baking powder

1 cup warm milk

1. Preheat oven to 200°C.
2. Combine flour, salt and baking powder.
3. Gradually add the milk until a soft dough forms.
4. Shape dough into a round loaf or 8 small rolls and place on a lined oven tray.
5. Bake for around 30–45 minutes, until the damper sounds hollow when tapped.

Herb and cheese damper

One night, after a long day of kids' sport, we came home to an emptyish cupboard and hungry kids, not to mention being uninspired and tired parents. Lizzie decided to give plain old damper a go. (If you could do it over a campfire, surely it must be simple.) Very quickly, she produced a herb, cheese and sundried-tomato loaf, and a plain loaf that we ate with some strawberry 'jam' (she made this by simply stewing some frozen strawberries with a little dextrose while the damper was cooking). The meal went down a treat. Now we tend to use this recipe to make herb rolls to eat with soup rather than as a meal (bread in itself isn't the most nutritious main meal option for kids, even if it is seed-oil and fructose-free). You can flavour the damper with herbs of your choice, and vary the amount of sundried tomato as you wish. Or experiment with your own flavourings.

Makes 1 loaf or 8 rolls

300 g self-raising flour

1 teaspoon salt

60 g butter, softened

½ cup tasty cheese, grated

¼ cup oregano leaves,
    finely chopped

4 sundried tomatoes,
    finely chopped

up to 180 ml milk,
    plus extra for glaze

2 tablespoons parmesan,
    grated

1. Preheat oven to 180°C.
2. Sift flour and salt into a bowl, then rub in the butter with your fingertips until the mix has the appearance of breadcrumbs.
3. Stir in the cheese, oregano and sundried tomatoes.
4. In a separate bowl, dilute the milk with ¼ cup of water.

5. Make a well in the centre of the dry ingredients and slowly add fluid until dough comes together (not all fluid may be required).

6. Turn dough out onto a floured surface and knead gently for a minute.

7. Shape dough into a round loaf or 8 small rolls and place on a lined oven tray. Brush with milk and sprinkle the top with parmesan cheese.

8. Baking time will vary according to the thickness of your damper. Lizzie's tend to take 45 minutes for a loaf and about 30 minutes for rolls, but you're after a lovely golden-coloured loaf that sounds hollow when tapped.

9. Tastes best served warm, so no need to wait.

Chips

When I was a young child, hot chips were a rarity. The only place that sold them was the local sandwich shop, and the only people who bought anything there were the teenagers rebelliously chomping on a fried snack between meals. The only time I ate chips was when my mum went to the trouble of chopping up potatoes and frying them in olive oil on the stove (a very occasional treat). In the four decades since then, Australian society has changed dramatically. Now there are more places selling hot chips than we could ever need. Most people would no more consider making their own than they would consider building their own cars. The art of deep-frying – let alone in animal fat – has become a dark mystery. But I like chips and I wasn't about to give them up easily. Not one of the thousands of hot-chip retailers in our neck of the woods fries in olive oil or animal fat. They all proudly display signs saying things like 'We only use cholesterol-free vegetable oil' or 'We fry in cottonseed oil for your health'. So, since shop-bought chips are out of the question, I was left with only one choice – fry my own.

First, I had to acquire the equipment. I searched the local department store for fryers and pored over their back-of-box instructions. They all seemed to insist that frying only occur in vegetable oil. I wondered whether this was a mechanical issue (would animal fat break the equipment?) or health advice, but couldn't find any answers on the packaging. In the end, I threw caution to the wind and bought one.

Next, I plundered the solid-fat section (just next to the butter) of the local supermarket. It was all a bit of a mystery and we first tried using lard, but it is relatively expensive and gives off a distinct odour. The best option is solidified cooking oil, which is blended animal fats; it cooks without any noticeable odour and produces the same crispy results.

When I followed the deep-fryer directions for vegetable oil, using solid fat instead, nothing broke, blew up or caught fire, so I can only conclude that the warnings to use vegetable oil were out of concern for my health. In fact, the whole process was quite easy, and the results were well worth the effort. If you want to try these recipes but don't have a deep-fryer or don't want to use animal fat, just do what my mum did: whack a large saucepan on the stove, fill it with extra light olive oil and crank the burner up to flat-out. Remember, you can re-use this oil several times if you sieve it to remove any bits of food once it has cooled, and store it in the fridge.

Traditional chips

2 kg solidified cooking oil or   potatoes (I usually allow one
   2 litres extra light olive oil   large potato per person –
                             King Edwards are the best)

1. Put enough oil to cover the potatoes in the deep-fryer and turn to
    80% of maximum heat (about 160°C).
2. Peel the potatoes (you can leave the skins on if you want them
    American-style). Cut into chip shapes; this is immeasurably easier if
    you get a potato chipper from your local kitchenware store.
3. Parboil chips until soft when pricked with a fork (usually 5–10
    minutes, depending on size) but not so soft that they break apart.
4. Dry (with paper towel) and cool (preferably in a fridge or freezer).
5. After checking that the cooking fat has reached the set heat,
    deep-fry (using the chip basket if you have one) until a little colour
    starts to appear.
6. Dump chips onto paper towel and allow to cool back to room
    temperature.
7. Deep-fry chips again at full heat (190°–200°C) until golden brown.
8. Dump chips back onto clean paper towel, then add salt (and
    vinegar if you like) to taste.

If you don't feel like doing all this in one night, you can freeze the
chips in advance. After the first frying, and once they have cooled,
place the chips in a plastic freezer bag. Then, when you want to
use them, pull them out and do the final fry (no need to thaw first).
This method works just as well and means you can pre-fry a large
quantity, freeze them and use smaller batches as needed. They will
stick together when you take them out of the freezer (but separate
in the fryer), so freeze them in fryer-capacity-sized batches.

No-hassle chips

2 kg solidified cooking oil or 2 litres extra-light olive oil

1 kg bag of frozen chips (see page 90 for the best ones)

1. Put appropriate amount of oil in deep-fryer and turn to maximum heat (190–200° C).
2. Ignore all cooking suggestions (such as oven-fry) on the chips bag.
3. Deep-fry at full heat until golden-brown.
4. Dump onto paper towel and season to taste.

Batters and crumbs

I haven't invented anything here. Most batters don't use sugar or any kind of fat. If you have a favourite recipe then use that or just ask Mr Google. For convenience, here are the ones I've used – I know they work.

Beer batter

Despite its name and the ingredients, this batter neither tastes like beer, nor is it alcoholic (the alcohol cooks off). It is especially good wrapped around a barramundi fillet. If you don't have beer, or don't want to use it in your food, use soda water instead.

Makes enough to coat 4 large fish fillets

1 large egg

1½ cups self-raising flour

1 bottle of beer (375 ml) or the same quantity of soda water, chilled

1. Whisk egg and combine with flour.
2. Stir in beer (or soda water) until you have a smooth batter.
3. Let the batter rest for half an hour in the fridge before using.

Tempura batter

This recipe is similar to the beer batter but makes a lighter and crispier batter, which I have started to prefer.

Makes enough to coat 4 large fillets

1 large egg

1 cup iced water or, preferably,
   crushed ice

1 cup plain flour

pinch of bicarbonate of soda

1. Whisk the egg and combine with the water or ice.
2. Add the flour and bicarbonate of soda, stirring until you have a smooth batter. Use immediately.

Battered food

Now that you have a batter, you are ready to deep-fry fish, chicken, onions (or tropical fruit if you are that way inclined). After some trial and error, I've worked out the following method to guarantee perfect fried food. In general, you want whatever you're battering to be about 1 cm thick. That's how fish fillets come, so no work required there, but if you're battering chicken breast, you'll need to beat it with a rolling pin to decrease its thickness.

1. Remove the chip basket from your deep-fryer – you don't want it getting in the way. Place fat in fryer and turn on to maximum heat (about 200°C).
2. Place a bowl of flour (any kind will do) next to the bowl of batter, which is next to your fryer.
3. Designate a 'dry' hand and a 'wet' hand. (I work from left to right so my dry hand is my left hand.)
4. With your dry hand, dunk the fillet in the flour, making sure it is well coated – the batter will only stick to food that is covered in flour.
5. Using your dry hand, drop the fillet into the batter, then retrieve it using your wet hand and hold it over the batter bowl to drain off any excess.
6. Using your wet hand, hold the fillet by one end and slowly lower it into the hot fat, moving it from side to side as you do. DO NOT just drop it in as it will splatter and the batter will fall off.
7. Cook fillet until golden brown and floating (raw meat doesn't float), then fish out with a slotted spoon or tongs and drip-dry over the fat.
8. Place fillet on a cake-drying rack briefly, to allow any excess oil to drip off (it's best to position the rack over some paper towel to save your benchtop), before serving.

Anthony's crumbs

Many people (including most of our children) prefer crumbed food to battered. Due to overwhelming demand from his siblings, my son Anthony developed this crumb recipe, which he now whips up every Sunday night as his deep-fried dinner. We make our breadcrumbs by shoving any leftover stale bread in the oven to dry and then whizzing it in a food processor. Plain white yeasted bread works best. Crumbing shortens the life of your cooking oil. You will get fewer cycles out of it (three or four) if you are crumbing each time because the crumbs dirty the oil much more than a batter or chips alone.

Serves 8 adults (makes enough crumb for 3 half chicken breasts or about 1 kg of chicken)

2 teaspoons black peppercorns	2¼ cups breadcrumbs (fresh)
1 tablespoon mixed herbs	4 eggs
1½ teaspoons salt	¾ cup plain flour

1. Remove the chip basket from your deep-fryer. Place fat in fryer and turn on to maximum heat (about 200°C).
2. Combine peppercorns, herbs and salt in a mortar and pestle, and grind finely.
3. In a bowl, combine the ground mixture with breadcrumbs by hand.
4. In a separate bowl, whisk eggs.
5. Sift flour into another bowl.
6. Line up your ingredients in this order: food to be deep-fried, bowl of flour, bowl of egg, bowl of crumb mixture, then deep-fryer.
7. Designate a 'dry' hand and a 'wet' hand. (I work from left to right so my dry hand is my left hand.)

8. With your dry hand, dunk the food in the flour, making sure it is well coated.

9. . Using your dry hand, drop the food into the egg, then retrieve it using your wet hand and hold it over the egg bowl to drain off any excess.

10. Using your wet hand, drop the food into the crumb mix and cover it well before removing it.

11. Using your wet hand, hold the food by one end and slowly lower it into the hot fat, moving it from side to side as you do. DO NOT just drop it in as it will splatter and the crumbs will fall off.

12. Cook until golden-brown and floating (raw meat doesn't float), then fish out with a slotted spoon or tongs and drip-dry over the fat.

13. Place food on a cake-drying rack (it's best to position this over some paper towel to save your benchtop).

Chicken schnitzel

Not everyone has, or wants, a deep-fryer. Before we discovered the joys of frying in animal fat, Lizzie would make this version of oven-baked chicken schnitzel for special occasions. It is a little time-consuming, but the schnitzels freeze really well after they've been cooked, so you can make a big batch and have some for another time; all you need to do is resuscitate them in a frying pan when you want to use them. Feel free to experiment with the recipe – try parmesan instead of tasty cheese, different herbs, garlic, some chilli, or whatever you like.

Serves 8

2 cups breadcrumbs

2 cups cheddar cheese, grated

2 teaspoons mixed (or dried Italian) herbs

2 eggs, lightly beaten

4 chicken breast fillets

60 g butter, melted

1. Preheat oven to 180°C. Line an oven tray with non-stick baking paper.
2. In a flat-based bowl or dish, mix together the breadcrumbs, cheese and herbs.
3. Place the eggs in a separate bowl.
4. Place the chicken fillets between two pieces of plastic wrap and flatten (bashing not rolling) with a rolling pin to a thickness of 1 cm. Cut the breasts in half (or smaller if you like).
5. Using one hand (your 'wet' hand), dip each chicken piece into the beaten egg and place into the dry mix.
6. Using your other hand (your 'dry' hand), cover the chicken in the breadcrumb mixture, then place on oven tray.
7. Once all chicken is coated, spoon over the butter.
8. Bake in the oven for 15–20 minutes until golden brown and cooked through.

Hash browns

This is another recipe you can personalise. You could add onion or herbs, and you can make them huge and thin (the size of the base of your frying pan) or cook them in a ring mould. Simply keep in mind that, of course, the cooking time will be altered by the thickness of your hash brown. This recipe doesn't use flour so is gluten-free.

Serves 8

8 potatoes, preferably Desiree (red-skinned)

1 egg, lightly beaten

salt and pepper to taste

olive oil for frying

1. Grate the potato (skin on). Place gratings in the centre of a tea towel, then bring the corners of the tea towel up and twist them together, wringing all the juice out of the potato.
2. Place potato in a bowl, and mix through the egg and seasoning.
3. Heat your frying pan to moderate heat and grease with a small amount of olive oil.
4. Place dollops of the potato mix on the hot frying pan, pushing it down with the back of an egg flip. Cook for 8–10 minutes or until coloured and cooked through.
5. Flip hash brown and cook for a similar time on the other side. Remove from pan and keep warm.
6. Continue until all the mixture is used.

Pestos, sauces and dips

It is almost impossible to find a commercial pesto, sauce or dip that isn't based on seed oils. Indeed, for many it is the primary ingredient. If you are lucky enough to have a supplier that bases their products on olive oil, you don't need this section. For the rest of us who like a good sauce, here are a few simple, quick and easy recipes that mean you don't have to go without.

Basil pesto

I believe that this will freeze for up to four months in an airtight container, and that to thaw it, you simply transfer it into the fridge for a few hours. The best we have managed is two-and-a-half months, because we love this stuff. It's great on pasta, in sandwiches, or (my favourite) on a bit of homemade sourdough toast. It's not critical to the recipe, but Lizzie goes the whole hog and grows her own basil for pesto. She's found 'Boxwood basil' (available at your local garden centre) the easiest variety to grow and harvest.

Makes approximately 350 ml

¼ cup pine nuts

1½ cups basil leaves

2 small garlic cloves

¾ cup grated parmesan

100 ml olive oil,

plus extra to seal

salt and pepper to taste

1. Toast the pine nuts (careful, they burn quickly) in a frying pan or for a few minutes in the oven at 180°C. Cool.
2. Process nuts, basil, garlic and parmesan in a food processor until finely chopped.

3. With motor still running, gradually add olive oil in a thin, steady stream until well combined.
4. Season as required with salt and pepper.
5. Transfer to an airtight container, covering with a thin layer of olive oil. Seal and refrigerate or freeze.

Sundried tomato pesto

This tastes great on bread and toast or stirred through pasta. We've even used it on pizza instead of tomato paste (for adults – our kids are not fans). It keeps well in the fridge in an airtight container.

Makes approximately 1½ cups

⅓ cup pine nuts

¾ cup sundried tomatoes
(choose carefully; the
Greenland brand I use is
not stored in oil)

2 garlic cloves, chopped

⅔ cup extra virgin olive oil
(if your sundried tomatoes
are stored in olive oil, you
may require only ½ cup)

⅓ cup finely grated parmesan

salt and pepper to taste

1. Toast the pine nuts (careful, they burn quickly) in a frying pan or for a few minutes in the oven at 180°C. Cool.
2. Process tomatoes, nuts and garlic in a food processor until almost smooth.
3. With motor still running, gradually add olive oil in a thin, steady stream until well combined.
4. Stir through parmesan (with motor off).
5. Season as required with salt and pepper.
6. Transfer to an airtight container, covering with a thin layer of olive oil. Seal and refrigerate or freeze.

Tatjana's flatbread

There's not much point giving you dip recipes without something to dip in the dip. Lizzie picked this one up from Tatjana, our school tuckshop convenor. She isn't your normal canteen lady; she makes everything from scratch, often relying on recipes from her Hungarian heritage. This recipe is yummy with dips. We've also found that it works as a thin and crispy pizza dough, if you don't have any yeast. (Divide the dough into four parts only.)

Makes 14

1 cup plain flour

1 cup self-raising flour

½ tablespoon salt

1 cup water

1 tablespoon olive oil

1. In a bowl, combine flours and salt.
2. Put water and oil in a jug.
3. Make a well in the centre of the dry ingredients and slowly add the water mixture. Mix into a dough.
4. Turn dough out onto a lightly floured surface and knead until smooth. Set aside (if you have time) for 15–20 minutes.
5. Divide dough into 14 pieces, rolling each into a thin round.
6. Heat a frying pan to a high heat, then turn down to medium. If desired, wipe the pan with a small amount of olive oil (for flavour).
7. Cook each round for 1–2 minutes, flipping once it bubbles and spots, to cook on the other side.
8. Keep breads warm as you cook the rest, then serve fresh.

Egyptian red beetroot dip

This recipe uses raw beetroot, something that had never before made its way into our shopping trolley (I didn't even know our supermarket sold it). We had always bought our beetroot in tins but had to stop doing so because it contains so much added sugar. Rather than learn how to pickle beetroot, we had simply deleted it from the menu, although our burgers suffered.

Lizzie made this dip the afternoon before it was needed and I think it added to the flavour. Tweak it to your taste; you might like more garlic, or different herbs (fresh mint or dill, perhaps?), or no herbs. Serve with dipping crackers and vegetable sticks.

Makes approximately 400 ml

2 (large) or 3 (small) beetroots – about 500 g	¼ teaspoon ground cumin
⅔ cup Greek yoghurt	¼ teaspoon ground coriander
1 clove garlic, crushed	¼ teaspoon ground cinnamon
2 tablespoons lemon juice	¼ teaspoon paprika
1 tablespoon extra virgin olive oil	salt and pepper to taste

1. If your beetroots have stems, cut them 1 cm from the beets. Clean carefully, trying not to nick the skin (otherwise the beets will leach colour).
2. Cook beetroots in a large saucepan of boiling salted water for 40–60 minutes until tender (test with a skewer). Drain and cool slightly, until they are easy to handle.
3. Wearing rubber gloves to prevent your hands from staining, rub the skins off the beetroots.

4. Chop skinned beetroots then place in a food processor. Add yoghurt, garlic, lemon juice, olive oil and herbs, and process to desired consistency.
5. Season with salt and pepper to taste.
6. Refrigerate until needed.

Hummus

Hummus is my kind of recipe: easy, forgiving, requires no fiddly ingredients and, of course, delicious. If you have a tin of chickpeas and a reasonably stocked pantry, you're most of the way there. This recipe tastes great whether you make it the day before or the day you need it.

Makes approximately 400 ml

1 x 400 g tin chickpeas, drained (reserve the liquid in case you want to loosen the consistency of your hummus)

1 garlic clove, crushed

2 tablespoons extra virgin olive oil

2 tablespoons lemon juice (if you are squeezing your own and you like an extra zing, you may wish to add a little of the zest, too)

1 teaspoon ground cumin (optional)

flat-leaf parsley, chopped (if you have it, as it adds a lovely freshness)

salt and pepper to taste

1. Blend or process the chickpeas, gradually adding garlic, olive oil, lemon juice, cumin and parsley.
2. Check seasoning, and add liquid (reserved from the tin) to achieve your desired consistency.
3. Refrigerate until serving.

Baba ghanoush (eggplant and tahini dip)

Eggplant is another vegetable we hadn't had much to do with until Lizzie volunteered at the local school's kitchen-garden program. But what a discovery – yum! For this recipe, the eggplant should ideally be chargrilled to provide a smoky flavour, but we don't have a chargrill pan, so we just roast it in the oven. (If you've got all the gear, you could brush your eggplant with olive oil and grill for 3–5 minutes per side instead.) This seems to be tastier if you make it the day before you need it, but it's still good if you whip it up and take it straight to the table.

The recipe uses tahini paste, which is about 28 per cent polyunsaturated fat, but you are using only 22 grams of tahini. Your end product will contain about 6 grams of polyunsaturated fat. If you plan on eating the entire batch yourself in one sitting or over the course of a day, you should (and can) leave the tahini paste out, creating more of an eggplant puree.

Makes approximately 350 ml

1 large eggplant	1 clove garlic, crushed
4 tablespoons lemon juice	2 tablespoons flat-leafed
1½ tablespoons tahini paste	parsley (finely chopped if
½ tablespoon extra virgin	not using a food processor)
olive oil	salt and pepper to taste

1. Preheat oven to 200°C. Line a baking tray with foil.
2. Wash eggplant and place it, wet, on the foil. Bake for 25–30 minutes, turning occasionally (you are trying to attain a smoky flavour, so the skin should be quite black but the flesh soft).

3. Allow eggplant to cool, then cut in half and scoop the flesh into a bowl, discarding the skin.

4. Pour lemon juice over the eggplant.

5. Process the eggplant (or cut it finely) with the tahini, olive oil, garlic and parsley.

6. Season with salt and pepper once desired consistency is achieved.

7. Refrigerate until ready to serve.

8. Taste again and adjust with more lemon juice, salt and/or pepper if you like before serving.

Tzatziki

I love tzatziki. The fresh taste goes with everything. This recipe is quick and simple, and our kids love helping to make it.

Makes approximately 350 ml

1 large cucumber

1 cup Greek yoghurt

1 small garlic clove, crushed

1 teaspoon finely chopped mint

½ tablespoon olive oil

salt and pepper to taste

1. Peel cucumber, slice in half lengthways and remove seeds with a spoon.
2. Coarsely grate cucumber and squeeze out any excess liquid.
3. Place yoghurt in a bowl and mix in cucumber, garlic, mint and oil.
4. Season to taste.
5. Refrigerate until ready to serve.

Guacamole

What dips section would be complete without a guacamole recipe? The problem is, I don't have one. I like my guacamole simple and fresh. I mash up an avocado and add lemon or lime juice to taste (with the added benefit that it keeps the avocado from going brown), salt and pepper to taste, and, if we have any, some chopped coriander leaves. If you like, you could add some chopped onion, some chopped and de-seeded tomato, and even some chilli. If you want your guacamole to stretch a bit further (hey, avocados are expensive), just add a little sour cream to the mix.

Tomato salsa

I first had this at kitchen-garden class at our kids' primary school. There wasn't a formal recipe and it's all about making it to your own taste. Lizzie often serves it with goat's cheese feta crumbled over the top and ample bread for a very popular weekend lunch at home. This amount was good for 25 bruschetta and easily satisfied our whole herd.

Makes 500 g

½ red onion, diced

5 large Roma tomatoes
(although any nice red
tomatoes will work)

juice of 1 lime

handful of coriander and mint
(to taste), finely chopped

salt and pepper to taste

1. Place onion in a bowl.
2. Dice the tomatoes, seeds and all, and add them to the onion.
3. Stir through the lime juice thoroughly, then add herbs.
4. Add salt and pepper to taste.

Semi-dried tomatoes

There is only one widely available brand of sundried tomato that is not sold in a seed oil (Greenland, sold in vacuum-sealed packs). You can use these in pesto but they're a little too dry for a salad. Our local greengrocer often has discount one-kilo packs of Roma tomatoes, so Lizzie decided to dry her own. It was remarkably simple and the outcome was delicious. They will keep for 2 weeks in the fridge or about a month in the freezer.

Makes around 1 kilogram

1 kg Roma tomatoes (or you could use any small tomato)	thyme leaves salt and pepper to taste extra virgin olive oil to cover

1. Preheat oven to 150°C.
2. Line a baking tray with non-stick baking paper.
3. Place an oven-safe wire rack on the prepared tray. (If you don't have one, don't worry, but cooking may take longer as it helps the drying process.)
4. Wash and cut the tomatoes in half lengthways, arranging them cut-side up on the tray (or on the wire rack, if you're using one).
5. Sprinkle with thyme leaves, and season with salt and pepper.
6. Bake in the oven for around 2½ hours (this is only a guide as cooking time depends on the size of the tomato, your oven and your desired drying result).
7. Once the tomato is dry around the edges but still soft in the middle, leave on the tray and set aside to cool.
8. Store in an airtight container, covering the tomatoes with extra virgin olive oil.

Dressings

We usually dress salads pretty simply at home, so this section is not so much about recipes as ideas. The very best day-to-day dressing is a simple lemon and olive oil mix. We usually start with two parts olive oil to one part lemon juice, and add salt and pepper to taste. You can add herbs to this mix, or add them to the salad so they are just touched by the dressing rather than left soaking in it.

One of the best-tasting simple dressings you can make is basically virgin olive oil and wholegrain mustard (check the ingredients of your mustard; some have added sugar but if it's under 3 grams per 100 grams it's fine to use). The most important thing about this dressing is that, since it contains no emulsifiers, it must be made – or at least shaken well – immediately before use, and must be tossed through the salad just before serving. (You don't want to get a big clump of mustard in one mouthful and undressed salad in the next.) It seems to work best on a four-to-one ratio of olive oil to mustard. If this is not fancy enough, you can always add vinegar or lemon juice and of course salt and pepper.

Greek yoghurt is a very handy thing to have in the fridge when it comes to salad dressings. (We tend to buy large quantities of it because the kids have taken to eating it with a bit of dextrose and vanilla essence for an afternoon treat before sport.) If you mix a little curry powder through it, the yoghurt makes a great accompaniment to a chicken salad. Adjust to suit your taste but begin with 1 teaspoon of curry powder to every 2 tablespoons of yoghurt. Another easy addition to a simple yoghurt dressing is some finely chopped mint leaves (and perhaps some crushed garlic, if you are in the mood).

Mayonnaise

We have a son who loves his chicken, lettuce and mayo roll for school lunch. When we discovered that there is no such thing as mayo made without seed oil (at least, not in our local supermarkets), we were in big trouble. Luckily, it turns out that mayo is not hard to make. Teenagers hate change, so Lizzie just refilled the old shop-bought whole-egg mayo jar and put it back in the fridge. It wasn't until he saw her making the next batch that he cottoned on to the change. It has since been christened 'Trickery mayo'. This recipe keeps well in the fridge.

Makes 700 ml

2 whole eggs

1 tablespoon Dijon mustard

2 tablespoons (or a little extra)
    lemon juice

2 cups light olive oil
    (extra virgin has too strong
    a taste for this recipe)

salt and pepper to taste

1. In a food processor, pulse eggs, mustard and lemon juice.
2. Slowly (whilst processing) add olive oil until mixture thickens.
3. Taste and season if required.
4. Transfer to a sealed container (an old mustard jar works a treat) and refrigerate.

Once you have the basic mayo recipe, you can trick it up for different dishes. Add a couple of minced garlic cloves, a dessertspoon of lemon juice and a pinch of salt to 1 cup of mayo and you have basic aioli. If fish is on the menu, add the following to 1 cup of mayo to make tartare sauce: 1 finely chopped small onion, 2 chopped dill pickles (or perhaps some chopped gherkin), a splash of lemon juice, 1 tablespoon chopped flat-leaf parsley, 1 teaspoon chopped chives, and salt and pepper to taste.

Snacks

Our two teenage sons took up rowing and eating as their summer hobbies and Lizzie has had to come up with a range of nutritious snacks to keep them going throughout the day. Here are recipes for the most popular ones.

Sausage rolls with tomato sauce

Our original recipe, which appeared in *Toxic Oil*, made about 32 party-sized rolls. But for one party Lizzie made them bite-sized – about 2 cm long – and the mix made more than 100. She was a bit worried that the reduced meat to pastry ratio would affect the taste, but it seemed to work. She really babysat them in the oven, turning them over once the base had browned and then putting them on their ends to make sure they were thoroughly cooked through. This had the added benefit of eliminating sogginess. She froze them after cooking, then reheated them (for about 15 minutes in a 160°C oven) before our guests arrived. (Party-sized rolls would take longer than this to heat through.)

**Makes about 100 bite-sized or 32 party-sized rolls
and about 100 ml tomato sauce**

2 small onions, diced

½ red capsicum, seeded
and diced

1 carrot, grated

1 zucchini, grated

600 g beef mince
(or pork if you prefer)

2 eggs, lightly beaten,
plus 1 extra, lightly
beaten, for glazing

2 tablespoons finely chopped
flat-leaf parsley

1 teaspoon mixed dried herbs

1 teaspoon pepper

½–⅔ cup breadcrumbs

4 sheets frozen butter puff
pastry, thawed

Tomato sauce

125 ml tomato passata

salt and pepper to taste

½ garlic clove, peeled

1–2 basil leaves

1. Start by making the tomato sauce. Bring the passata to the boil in a small saucepan over medium heat.

2. Stir in the salt, pepper, garlic and basil leaves to taste.

3. Continue cooking until the mixture reaches the right consistency, bearing in mind that it will thicken when chilled.

4. Remove from the heat. Remove the garlic and basil leaves, then set the sauce aside to cool. Pour into a bottle and refrigerate until needed.

5. To make the sausage rolls, preheat oven to 200°C for bite-sized rolls or 220°C for larger rolls.

6. Cook the onion, capsicum, carrot and zucchini in a medium frying pan over low heat to reduce the moisture content. Cool then pat with paper towel to reduce the moisture content further.

7. In a bowl, combine the mince, two eggs, parsley, herbs, pepper and breadcrumbs. Add the vegetables and mix well.

8. Lay a sheet of puff pastry on the benchtop.

9. If making bite-sized rolls, you will make five long rolls from each sheet of puff pastry and cut each into at least five and as much as ten. If making party-sized rolls, you will make two rolls from each sheet and cut each into four. Place a band of mixture along one edge of the sheet of puff pastry, leaving a 1 cm border along the edge. Roll until mixture is covered, brush about 1 cm of the free edge with water (to help the pastry stick and seal), then roll on top and cut. Continue until you've used all the pastry and mixture. Leave each roll sitting on its join.

10. Baste each roll with the remaining beaten egg, then cut into evenly bite-sized or party-sized pieces.

11. Bake, seam-side down, for 20–25 minutes or until golden and puffed. (We turn ours over halfway through the cooking time and even turn the bite-sized rolls on their ends.)

12. Serve the rolls hot, with chilled tomato sauce.

Stewed tomato sauce

This is not strictly speaking a sauce, but we use it like one, since commercial tomato sauces are out of the question. This is another use for cheap bags of tomatoes. Lizzie often cooks this up to go with sausage rolls. Or, for brekkie, she might throw some tinned cannellini beans in with the sauce for what our kids have christened 'faked beans'. You might like to throw in some garlic and chilli, add some capsicum, or change the herbs to personalise it. If you want a really smooth sauce run it through a food processor for a few seconds.

Makes approximately 500 ml

1 tablespoon olive oil

1 large onion, diced

1 kg tomatoes, diced roughly

chopped oregano, parsley and chives

salt and pepper to taste

1. Place a saucepan over medium heat, add olive oil and warm.
2. Add onion to pan to soften and colour slightly.
3. Add tomatoes, herbs, salt and pepper.
4. Lower heat, cover and cook, stirring occasionally (being careful that the tomato doesn't catch and burn) until the tomato softens. Remove from heat.
5. Check seasoning and serve. The 'sauce' is best served warm, but can be stored in the fridge in an airtight container for up to a week.

Meat pies

Like most of the recipes in this book, it's really more about being organised and prepared than actual chef stuff. For pies, you can buy pre-diced beef (or whatever meat you want to use) at most supermarkets and butchers. Don't pay for expensive meat because you are going to boil it soft. And the more fat it has in it, the better the flavour will be. Simply sear it then simmer it in stock for a few hours and you have instant filling. Use a shop-bought puff-pastry case made with butter, such as Carème Butter Puff Pastry or Pampas Butter Puff, and you have a pie in minutes.

The best news is that the pie filling freezes really well, so if you knock up a big batch of filling one lazy Sunday afternoon, you're set for pies whenever the mood takes you. Once you've got a freezer full of filling and puff-pastry sheets, assembling a pie requires barely more effort than taking a frozen pie out of the same freezer. If you do it yourself and make sure the puff pastry you buy is made with butter rather than margarine, you will be consuming almost no polyunsaturated fats and you will know exactly what is in your pie. If you want to go the extra mile, then make sure the beef you use is grass-fed.

This recipe makes one large (25 cm) deep meat pie. It satisfies the eight of us (equivalent to four adults and four kids) when served with vegetables for dinner. We've also made it into single-serve pies. We tend to make up a batch of filling and freeze it, then thaw and make the pie with puff pastry just before we're going to eat it.

You could also make this gluten-free by exchanging the flour in the filling for a gluten-free alternative and creating a shepherd's pie with a mashed-potato top instead of a pastry-encased pie.

Serves 6

1 tablespoon olive oil

1 kg diced casserole beef, untrimmed

2 generous tablespoons Bonox (there, now you know what to use Bonox for)

3 heaped tablespoons plain flour

1 cup cold water, plus extra for cooking

2 sheets frozen butter puff pastry

1. Place a large saucepan over medium heat. Add olive oil to cover base.

2. Add beef and Bonox.

3. Meanwhile, in a separate bowl, gradually mix together flour and water, stirring until there are no lumps. Set aside.

4. Pour extra water into saucepan until meat is almost covered. Then add flour and water mix. Cover and bring to the boil. Allow to boil for 5 minutes, covered.

5. Uncover and simmer (stirring occasionally so meat doesn't catch on base of saucepan) for at least 2 hours or until meat has broken down and has a thick gravy-like consistency. Remove from heat. If you don't want to use the filling straight away, freeze it in an airtight container.

6. When ready to assemble, defrost filling if frozen. Preheat oven to 200°C. Grease a 25 cm pie tin.

7. Take the first sheet of puff pastry, place it in the pie dish and prick the bottom. (Store-bought puff pastry may be a bit smaller than your dish; roll it out a little, and cut and paste any overhang to where it is needed.)

8. Add filling on top of pastry. Place second sheet of pastry over the top and press into edges of the pie to attach to base.

9. If you want to get fancy, use the pastry off-cuts to make little decorations for the top of the pie.

10. Bake for 30–45 minutes or until golden brown. Serve.

Pie pastry

If you want to go the whole hog, you can make your own pastry. Give it a go at least once – it really isn't that hard, and the pay-off is worth the effort. This just here for the adventurers, there is no nutritional reason to prefer home-made to shop bought.

Makes three 25 cm square sheets

2½ cups plain flour, plus extra
for dusting
1 tablespoon dextrose
(optional)

1 teaspoon salt
225 g cold butter, grated
½–1 cup very cold water

1. Mix the flour, dextrose (if using) and salt in a large bowl.
2. Sprinkle the butter through the dry mix.
3. Drizzle in ½ cup water, then gently mix into the flour and butter using your fingers.
4. When the water is completely incorporated, add a little more at a time until the dough just comes together.
5. Once you have large clumps of pastry, use your hands to gently form your dough into a single piece.
6. Divide the dough in two (I make one slightly larger than the other for the base of the pie). Place each on a separate piece of cling wrap and wrap it up, using the sides of the cling wrap to press and shape the dough into a disc as you go. Refrigerate for 1 hour (preferably 2, but we rarely have time).
7. When you're ready to roll out your pastry, lightly dust your board or benchtop and rolling pin with flour. Roll out the pastry to the size you need, working gently; you want to keep visible lumps of butter in the finished product.

Crackers

When we stopped eating seed oils, Lizzie and I missed water crackers and the kids missed Barbecue Shapes. Lizzie has a butter-based cracker recipe but, as this book was being written, she began thinking about recipes made with good non-dairy alternatives. These biscuits (inspired by an online water crackers recipe on foodlovers.co.nz) are easy and have become a hit at our place. They also work with gluten-free flour (for 140 g wheaten flour, use 1 cup gluten-free flour plus arrowroot powder – 1 teaspoon for bread or ½ teaspoon in baking).

Lizzie sometimes adds dried mixed herbs with chilli, which packs a popular punch. Other toppings she's experimented with include herbs and parmesan, and salt flakes. These are easy and liked by all the family and, as such, we haven't strayed far from these successful flavour combinations.

200 g plain flour

1 teaspoon salt

100 ml cold water

2 tablespoons olive oil

(plus extra for brushing)

1. Preheat oven to 180°C. Line two baking trays with non-stick baking paper.
2. In a bowl, combine flour and salt. Make a well in the dry ingredients. Add water and olive oil, mixing together with a knife.
3. Once combined, knead dough on a lightly floured surface until smooth (approximately 5 minutes). Roll dough out as thinly as possible (I aim for a rough square 45 cm x 45 cm). Cut into desired shapes (for ease I use a pizza cutter).

4. Brush lightly with olive oil (and prick each biscuit several times with a fork if you want them flat). Lift one at a time onto prepared tray and sprinkle over toppings, if using.
5. Bake for around 15 minutes or until biscuits colour slightly.
6. Cool on a wire rack and store in an airtight container.

Savoury fritters

We always have meat leftover after a roast, and unfortunately not all our children like omelettes yet, so I revive a favourite from my youth and use up the leftovers with this savoury fritter recipe. We eat it with sour cream or homemade stewed tomato for brekkie, and leftovers are taken to school for lunch (two fritters, buttered, and with cheese in the middle like a sandwich). And if you still have fritters left over, they freeze well.

Makes 10 large fritters

300 g self-raising flour

1½ cups milk

3 eggs

olive oil or butter for greasing

1 cup frozen peas and corn

1 cup roast meat,

    finely chopped

Greek yoghurt, to serve

1. Place flour, milk and eggs in a large bowl and mix (I use an egg mixer) until you have a smooth batter.
2. Add the other ingredients and stir through.
3. Place a frying pan over medium heat and lightly grease with olive oil or butter.
4. Pour in the batter to form individual fritters, then flip when bubbles start to appear in the top. Continue until all batter is used, keeping the fritters warm until you are ready to serve.
5. Serve with a dollop of Greek yoghurt.

Olive oil rice malt biscuits

These crunchy biscuits may take a little longer to colour when baking (compared to butter) and require more thorough supervision, but they are very tasty and very popular.

Makes 12–14

100 ml olive oil
  (Lizzie uses mild)
½ cup rice malt syrup
1 cup plain flour

¼ teaspoon bicarbonate of soda
¼ teaspoon ground ginger
  or ½ teaspoon ground
  cinnamon

1. Preheat oven to 180°C and line two baking trays with non-stick baking paper.
2. Place olive oil and rice malt syrup in a saucepan over low heat and mix to combine.
3. Take off heat and add dry ingredients, mixing well until a smooth consistency.
4. Place dessertspoons of mixture onto prepared trays (well spaced as these biscuits spread), flattening with wet fingers or the back of a spoon – these biscuits are loveliest thin and crispy.
5. Bake for about 10 minutes (thickness of biscuits may vary timing) or until coloured but not dark (the biscuits will harden as they cool).
6. Cool on trays until biscuits start to harden, then transfer to a wire rack to cool completely.
7. Store in an airtight container (or freeze for school lunches).

Coconut oil chocolate biscuits

Once again, this is a recipe converted from using butter. When Lizzie was creating these, she found the only difficulty was that the coconut oil became solid as the mixture cooled – which required shaping the biscuit with a warm mixture (and asbestos hands). The solution? Working fast and using spoons to portion out the mixture onto trays. You can also replace the coconut oil with olive oil and add 1 tablespoon of dried milk powder to the dry ingredients.

Makes 12–14

100 g coconut oil

1 cup dextrose,
   plus extra for dusting

175 g plain flour

2 tablespoons cocoa

¼ teaspoon bicarbonate of soda

1. Preheat oven to 180°C and line two baking trays with non-stick baking paper.
2. Melt coconut oil in a saucepan over medium heat. Add dextrose and stir occasionally until dissolved (do not boil). It will separate, but be patient as it eventually comes together.
3. Turn heat to low and add all dry ingredients, mixing until a smooth consistency.
4. Working quickly, scoop dessertspoons of the mixture onto the prepared trays (the cooler the mixture, the more rustic and cracked the top. Flatten biscuits with wet fingers or the back of a spoon. These biscuits don't spread while cooking, so flatten to the desired thickness.
5. Bake for 10–15 minutes or until coloured but not dark (the biscuits will harden as they cool).
6. Cool on trays until biscuits begin to harden, then transfer to a wire rack to cool completely.
7. Dust with dextrose and store in an airtight container (or freeze for school lunches).

Olive oil oat biscuits

The inspiration for these biscuits came from the Cobram Estate website. It takes but a small alteration to make these with dextrose and they are delicious. Lizzie uses a saucepan over low heat to mix the wet ingredients and bicarb soda. This is not essential. She simply finds it easier to mix them all when a little warm. If the mixture feels a little dry to roll into biscuit portions, wet your hands or add a dessertspoon of water to the final dough.

Makes 12–14

1 cup plain flour

1 cup dextrose

1 cup rolled oats

¾ cup desiccated coconut

4 tablespoons rice malt syrup

1½ tablespoons water

1 teaspoon bicarbonate of
   soda

⅔ cup olive oil
   (Lizzie uses mild)

1. Preheat oven to 175°C (155°C fan-forced) and line two baking trays with non-stick baking paper.
2. In a bowl, combine flour, dextrose, oats and coconut.
3. Stir the rice malt syrup and water together until combined.
4. Stir in bicarb.
5. Pour wet mixture into dry, stirring through olive oil until combined.
6. Roll mixture into balls.
7. Place on prepared trays and flatten with fork or heel of hand. These really spread, so place them well apart.
8. Bake for about 20 minutes or until golden.
9. Cool on wire rack and store in airtight container.

Olive oil cake

Lizzie found this recipe for an olive oil 'crazy cake' online and thought it would be fun to adapt. Crazy cakes (or WWII cakes) are made without milk, eggs or butter. Lizzie didn't expect it to become a favourite, but it has. At the time, Lizzie also wanted to trial icings made without butter, so this cake was on high rotation as a test base (see page 153). If you do choose to ice it, do so just before serving as the icing becomes quite hard when left for a day. If you don't want to ice the cake (Lizzie doesn't always), you can simply add extra dextrose to the batter as she's done here. This cake is lovely and moist, but if you want extra lightness, you can add an egg. This can also be made gluten-free, using the conversion on page 145.

1½ cups plain flour

1¼ cups dextrose (1 cup if
 using icing; see page 153)

1 teaspoon bicarbonate of soda

½ teaspoon salt

¼ cup cocoa, sifted,
 plus ½–1 tablespoon extra

1 cup water

⅓ cup olive oil, plus extra for
 brushing

1 tablespoon vinegar

1 egg, beaten (optional)

1. Preheat oven to 170°C (150°C fan-forced) and grease a loaf tin (mine is 22 cm x 11 cm).
2. In a large bowl, combine 1 cup flour, dextrose, baking soda, salt and cocoa.
3. In a smaller bowl, whisk together water, oil and vinegar (and egg if using).
4. Pour wet ingredients into dry ingredients, whisking until thoroughly combined, then pour into prepared tin.

5. Bake for 50–60 minutes or until a skewer inserted into the cake comes out clean.

6. Mix remaining ¼ cup dextrose with the extra cocoa, to taste.

7. Brush cake top with olive oil, then sprinkle with cocoa dextrose mix.

Vanilla cupcakes

When Lizzie made a vanilla version of this cake, it tasted good but she found it was tricky to bake evenly. So one of the kids suggested making cupcakes – and they worked a treat. Simply remove the cocoa (obviously), use 1 cup dextrose and add an extra ¼ cup flour (to make 1¾ cups) as well as 1 teaspoon of vanilla extract. Follow the method as above. Lizzie used patty pans, which produced a baker's dozen worth of little cakes. She baked them for around 20 minutes (but keep an eye on them past the 15-minute mark).

Coconut oil icing

When you're choosing a coconut oil for this recipe, you'll need to consider the flavour you want for your icing – some love a full-bodied coconut oil, while others prefer an oil with minimal coconut flavour and aroma.

¼ cup coconut oil, melted

1 cup dextrose

about ¼ cup warm water

2 tablespoons cocoa, sifted

1. Using an electric mixer, beat together oil and dextrose, adding water 1 tablespoon at a time until mixture is paste-like.
2. Add the cocoa. If needed, gradually add more water to reach the required consistency.
3. Spread icing over cake.
4. Serve immediately, or leave icing to harden (this will be faster in the fridge).

Olive oil icing

If getting out the mixer is a bridge too far for the coconut oil icing recipe on page 153, you can make an icing with olive oil instead.

1 cup dextrose

3 tablespoons olive oil

2 tablespoons cocoa, sifted

2–2½ tablespoons water

1. Place dextrose, oil and cocoa in a saucepan over low heat.
2. Gradually add the water, stirring thoroughly, until it reaches your desired consistency.
3. Use icing while still warm. It will firm as it cools.

Fake sustagen

I have some older relatives who've recently needed to spend time in hospital. Because it is important that they not lose weight, hospital dietitians provided them with free access to Sustagen. The idea is that these powdered milk drinks are an effective way to boost a patient's food intake without requiring them to eat huge meals. When they were discharged, the hospital dietitian recommended that they continue to order in bulk and consume Sustagen. I, of course, was keen to check that the product wasn't just lolly water. And much to my relief, I discovered that while Sustagen was about half sugar, it was pure glucose. Brilliant! All good. Until May 2016.

Because then Nestle decided to 'improve the nutritional profile' of Sustagen by replacing the glucose with cane sugar. Effectively this means they replaced half the nutritionally harmless glucose with toxic fructose. Needless to say, we cancelled our regular order immediately.

Luckily, however, Lizzie was able to knock up a recipe that emulates it perfectly. Now she mixes up bulk batches for our relatives and, while she's at it, she does an extra jar for our kids. There's nothing a kid who's just rowed 2 kilometres loves more than a long, tall glass of Fake Sustagen.

Before you start, you will need to make up a batch of vanilla dextrose. This is a handy thing to have around anyway. Vanilla makes the relatively non-sweet dextrose really zing.

Vanilla dextrose

Vanilla dextrose is simply vanilla beans blitzed with dextrose in a food processor. We bought beans in bulk to use in making vanilla essence and had some leftover. Lizzie cut 3 vanilla beans lengthways and scraped out the seeds, then chopped the beans into 1 cm pieces and threw them and the seeds into the food processor with a 1 kg bag of dextrose. Then she sieved the dextrose, put it in a jar, and threw the leftover bits back into the processor with another bag of dextrose. Then she repeated the sieving and storing (shaking the storage bottle up to even the concentration) – make sure you test that it is vanilla-ry enough though.

Then – even better – we discovered a method using hardened vanilla beans that would otherwise go to waste. We purchased a coffee grinder (less than $15 at Kmart) as we didn't have a small enough processor and used 2–3 hardened beans per 2 kg of dextrose, as above. It was a great result.

Vanilla fake sustagen

1 cup milk powder	¼ cup vanilla dextrose

Chocolate fake sustagen

1 cup milk powder	¼ cup sifted cocoa powder
½ cup dextrose	

To serve, mix 60 g of Fake Sustagen with 200 ml of milk.

Caramel corn puffs

These corn puffs are especially convenient for after-school, between-activities snacks. We used to make these with butter, but Lizzie wanted to see if they would work with olive oil. They did. While similar recipes use more than double the sweetener, we try for a slightly sweet, lighter, crispy bites. If you prefer more toffee, double the rice malt syrup. If these not as sweet as you would like, you can dust them with a bit of dextrose before storing them in an airtight container. We enjoy them as is. You'll find the corn puffs in the health-food aisle at the supermarket.

¼ cup olive oil

½ cup rice malt syrup

170 g corn puffs

1. Preheat oven to 180°C and line a baking tray with baking paper.
2. Combine the olive oil and rice malt syrup in a saucepan over medium heat, stirring until smooth (do not worry if it bubbles a little).
3. Take saucepan off heat and pour in corn puffs.
4. Stir until every corn puff is coated with the olive oil mixture.
5. Pour onto prepared tray, spreading out into an even layer.
6. Bake for around 15 minutes, or until starting to colour (you can stir them occasionally if you prefer a more even caramel colour).
7. Remove from oven – they will harden as they cool on the tray.
8. Store in an airtight container.

Desserts

Finally, a few recipes for the pudding hounds.

Churros

I thought we needed to try as least one sweet treat deep-fried in animal fat (just to be sure it could be done, you understand). We tried two different methods of cooking churros (Spanish doughnuts), and they both worked well but gave different results. Churros are usually served with a chocolate dipping sauce and the first recipe makes batons of dense, deep-fried batter that are perfect for dipping. The second recipe creates doughnuts that look and taste like the traditional doughnuts I remember; these are delicious dusted with a dextrose/cinnamon mix. (Dextrose is a powdered version of glucose that looks like sugar but doesn't contain the dangerous fructose. It is sold in one-kilo bags in the home-brew section of the supermarket. For more about dextrose, see *Eat Real Food*.)

Serves 4 (makes approximately 30 x 5 cm batons for dipping)

oil for deep-frying
(solidified animal fat
or extra light olive oil)
1 cup water
1 tablespoon butter
(or coconut oil)

1 teaspoon dextrose
¼ teaspoon salt
1 cup plain flour
¼ teaspoon baking powder

1. Heat the oil for deep-frying in a suitable cooking container (a deep-fryer if you have one, or a frying pan if you don't) to approximately 180°C (or until a cube of bread turns golden after 15 seconds of immersion).

2. Meanwhile, in a separate saucepan, combine water, butter, dextrose and salt. Bring to the boil over medium heat.

3. Put flour and baking powder in a bowl.

4. Slowly pour boiling water mixture over flour mixture, stirring constantly with a fork, until you achieve a smooth dough (sticky not runny) with no lumps.

5. Spoon dough into a pastry/icing bag and use the largest nozzle or leave the nozzle off completely, like I do.

6. Squeeze lengths of dough into the oil. (I like shorter lengths because they are strong enough for dipping, but you can also make longer churros and serve them with the sauce poured over.)

7. When golden-brown on both sides, remove churros from oil with a slotted spoon and drain on paper towel. Continue until all mixture is used.

8. Serve with hot fudge sauce (see over).

Hot fudge sauce

Serves 4 (on ice-cream, but you may want to double the mix depending on how you plan to serve this dish)

1 tablespoon butter

1 tablespoon cocoa

¼ cup dextrose

¼ cup thickened cream

½ teaspoon vanilla essence

1. Melt butter over low heat, then stir through the cocoa.
2. Add dextrose, stirring to dissolve.
3. Add cream and bring mixture to the boil for 1 minute, stirring continuously.
4. Remove from heat, add vanilla and mix well
5. Cool (sauce will thicken as it cools).
6. Store in fridge, warm to serve.

Dusted churros

Serves 4

1 cup water

100 g unsalted butter

1 cup plain flour

¼ teaspoon salt

3 eggs (or 2 extra-large),
  lightly whisked

oil for frying

1 cup dextrose

2 teaspoons ground cinnamon

1. Combine water and butter in a saucepan over high heat, boiling for a few minutes until butter melts. Remove from heat.
2. Add flour and salt, stirring with a wooden spoon. When well combined, put aside to cool.
3. In a shallow dish or bowl, mix the dextrose and cinnamon. Set aside for rolling the churros in after cooking.
4. Once cool, add the eggs one at a time, beating well after each addition, until smoothly combined.
5. Spoon dough into a piping bag with a large nozzle. (I have experimented with different-sized and shaped nozzles, as well as with no nozzle; the size and shape affects the cooking time and crispness/doughiness of the doughnuts, but all were enjoyable.)
6. Heat the frying oil in the deep-fryer or frying pan to approximately 180°C (or until a cube of bread turns golden after 15 seconds of immersion), then pipe desired lengths of dough into the hot oil (cutting dough from nozzle with a knife or clean pair of scissors). Cook 1–2 minutes, until golden-brown.
7. Remove from oil with a slotted spoon and drain on kitchen paper, continuing this process until all mixture is used.
8. Roll the churros in the cinnamon/dextrose mix to coat.
9. Serve warm.

Endnotes

These notes are not intended to be a comprehensive list of the resources I relied on. Instead, they highlight the major signposts for further reading. Many of the studies listed here refer to a library of earlier work and most of them are freely available for the curious nutritional detective. If there is something you just can't find, you can always ask me. The best place to ask (so everyone can see the answer) is on my Facebook page: business.facebook.com/sweetdavidg

1. Big fat lies

9. The Australian Government's Australian Guide . . .: National Health and Medical Research Council 2017, *Australian Guide to Healthy Eating*, Department of Health and Ageing, 1 May 2017, www.eatforhealth.gov.au/sites/default/files/content/The%20Guidelines/n55_agthe_large.pdf

11. There was just one journal paper . . .: I D Frantz Jr et al., 'Test of effect of lipid lowering by diet on cardiovascular risk. The Minnesota Coronary Survey.', *Arteriosclerosis*, Jan–Feb 1989, vol. 9, no. 1, pp. 129–135, doi.org/10.1161/01.ATV.9.1.129.

11. In 2016, investigators from the US . . .: C E Ramsden et al., 'Re-evaluation of the traditional diet-heart hypothesis: analysis of recovered data from Minnesota Coronary Experiment (1968-73)', *The BMJ*, 12 April 2016, vol. 353, i1246, doi.org/10.1136/bmj.i1246

11. The results backed up a similar . . .: C E Ramsden et al., 'Use of dietary linoleic acid for secondary prevention of coronary heart disease and death: evaluation of recovered data from the Sydney Diet Heart Study and updated meta-analysis', *The BMJ*, 5 February 2013, vol. 346, e8707, doi.org/10.1136/bmj.e8707

14. Unfortunately, we've just discovered that one . . .: R A Freeborn et al., 'The Immune Response to Influenza is Suppressed by the Synthetic Food Additive and Nrf2 Activator, *tert*-butylhydroquinone (tBHQ)', *The FASEB Journal*, April 2019, vol. 33, no. 1, www.fasebj.org/doi/10.1096/fasebj.2019.33.1_supplement.505.3

1. Polyunsaturated fats cause cancer

14. H Esterbauer et al., 'Chemistry and biochemistry of 4-hydroxynonenal, malonaldehyde and related aldehydes', *Free Radical Biology and Medicine*, 1991, vol. 11, no. 1, pp. 81–128, doi.org/10.1016/0891-5849(91)90192-6;
W A Pryor & J P Stanley, 'Suggested mechanism for the production of malonaldehyde during the autoxidation of polyunsaturated fatty acids: nonenzymic production of prostaglandin endoperoxides during autoxidation', *Journal of Organic Chemistry*, 1975, vol. 40, no. 24, pp. 3615–17, doi.org/10.1021/jo00912a038;
S Reuter et al., 'Oxidative stress, inflammation, and cancer: How are they linked?', *Free Radical Biology and Medicine*, 1 December 2010, vol. 49, no. 11, pp. 1603-1616, doi.org/10.1016/j.freeradbiomed.2010.09.006;
H Yin et al., 'Free radical lipid peroxidation: mechanisms and analysis', *Chemical Reviews*, 2011, vol. 111, no. 10, pp. 5944–72, doi.org/10.1021/cr200084z;
H Zhong & H Yin, 'Role of lipid peroxidation derived 4-hydroxynonenal (4-HNE) in cancer: focusing on mitochondria', *Redox Biology*, 2015, vol. 4, pp. 193–99, doi.org/10.1016/j.redox.2014.12.011

2. Polyunsaturated fats cause childhood cancers

15. Cancer Australia, 'Children's cancer: statistics', Australian Government, 2019, childrenscancer.canceraustralia.gov.au/about-childrens-cancer/statistics/pdf;
J Bu-Tian et al., 'Paternal Cigarette Smoking and the Risk of Childhood Cancer Among Offspring of Nonsmoking Mothers', *JNCI: Journal of the National Cancer Institute*, 5 February 1997, vol. 89, no. 3, pp. 238–243, doi.org/10.1093/jnci/89.3.238;

J Laubenthal et al., 'Cigarette smoke-induced transgenerational alterations in genome stability in cord blood of human F1 offspring', *The FASEB Journal*, October 2001, vol. 26, no. 10, pp. 3946–56, doi.org/10.1096/fj.11-201194

More detailed analysis of the evidence (with links to source studies): http://davidgillespie.org/how-avoiding-vegetable-oil-can-prevent-childhood-cancer/

3. Polyunsaturated fats help fructose cause heart disease

16. L Hooper et al., 'Dietary fat intake and prevention of cardiovascular disease: systematic review', *The BMJ*, March 2001, vol. 322, pp.757–63, doi.org/10.1136/bmj.322.7289.757;

    B Lamarche et al., 'Small, dense low-density lipoprotein particles as a predictor of the risk of Ischemic heart disease in men: prospective results from the Quebec Cardiovascular Study', *Circulation*, January 1997, vol. 95, no. 1, pp. 69–75, doi.org/10.1161/01.CIR.95.1.69;

    M Leosdottir, 'Dietary fat intake and early mortality patterns – data from the Malmö Diet and Cancer Study', *Journal of Internal Medicine*, August 2005, vol. 258, no. 2, pp. 153–165, doi.org/10.1111/j.1365-2796.2005.01520.x;

    D L McGee et al., 'Ten-Year Incidence of Coronary Heart Disease in the Honolulu Heart Program', *American Journal of Epidemiology*, 1984, vol. 119, no. 5, pp. 653–666, doi.org/10.1093/oxfordjournals.aje.a113787;

    R B Shekelle et al., 'Diet, serum cholesterol, and death from coronary heart disease: The Western Electric study', *New England Journal of Medicine*, 1981, vol. 304, no. 2, pp. 65–70, doi.org/10.1056/NEJM198101083040201

4. Polyunsaturated fats make you blind

17. Deloitte Access Economics, 'Eyes on the Future: A clear outlook on Age-related Macular Degeneration', Macular Disease Foundation Australia, Sydney, 2011, p. 12, www.mdfoundation.com.au/content/deloitte-access-economics-report-released-macular-degeneration

    More detailed analysis of the evidence (with links to source studies): http://davidgillespie.org/stop-it-or-youll-go-blind/

5. Polyunsaturated fats cause Parkinson's disease

17. More detailed analysis of the evidence (with links to source studies): D Gillespie, 'Every drop of vegetable oil takes us further along the path to Parkinson's disease', 2014, David Gillespie blog, davidgillespie.org/every-drop-of-vegetable-oil-takes-us-further-along-the-path-to-parkinsons-disease;

B C L Lai & J K C Tsui, 'Epidemiology of Parkinson's disease', *British Columbia Medical Journal (BCMJ)*, April 2001, vol. 43, no. 3, pp. 133–37, www.bcmj.org/articles/epidemiology-parkinson's-disease

6. Polyunsaturated fats give you rheumatoid arthritis

18. Australian Institute of Health and Welfare, 'A snapshot of rheumatoid arthritis', *AIHW Bulletin 116*, 2013, www.aihw.gov.au/reports/chronic-musculoskeletal-conditions/a-snapshot-of-rheumatoid-arthritis/contents/table-of-contents;
    Australian Institute of Health and Welfare, 'The burden of musculoskeletal conditions in Australia', 2011, www.aihw.gov.au/getmedia/eed9f208-1d28-439c-aeb8-93509641fc72/20908.pdf.aspx?inline=true
    More detailed analysis of the evidence (with links to source studies): http://davidgillespie.org/how-to-avoid-rheumatoid-arthritis-and-stop-your-kids-getting-it-too/

7. Polyunsaturated fats give you multiple sclerosis

19. A Jana & K Pahan, 'Oxidative stress kills human primary oligodendrocytes via neutral sphingomyelinase: implications for multiple sclerosis', *The Journal of Neuroimmune Pharmacology (JNIP)*, March 2007, vol. 2, no. 2, pp. 184–93, www.ncbi.nlm.nih.gov/pmc/articles/PMC2131733/
    More detailed analysis of the evidence (with links to source studies): http://davidgillespie.org/margarine-seed-oil-filled-brothers-give-us-multiple-sclerosis/

8. Polyunsaturated fats give you osteoporosis

20. Osteoporosis Australia Medical and Scientific Advisory Committee, 'What is it?', Osteoporosis Australia, 7 February 2014, www.osteoporosis.org.au
    More detailed analysis of the evidence (with links to source studies): http://davidgillespie.org/how-margarine-breaks-your-bones/

9. Polyunsaturated fats cause allergies and asthma

20. Australasian Society of Clinical Immunology and Allergy Inc. (ASCIA), *Allergy and Immune Diseases in Australia (AIDA) Report 2013*, Sydney, 2013, www.allergy.org.au/images/stories/reports/ASCIA_AIDA_Report_2013.pdf;
    T Dunder et al., 'Diet, serum fatty acids, and atopic diseases in childhood', *Allergy*, 2001, vol. 56, no. 5, pp. 425–28, doi.org/10.1034/j.1398-9995.2001.056005425.x;

W K Liew et al., 'Anaphylaxis fatalities and admissions in Australia', *The Journal of Allergy and Clinical Immunology*, 2009, vol. 123, no. 2, pp. 434–42, www.jacionline.org/article/S0091-6749(08)01929-5/fulltext;

S Sausenthaler et al., 'Margarine and butter consumption, eczema and allergic sensitization in children: the LISA birth cohort study', *Pediatric Allergy and Immunology*, 2006, vol. 17, no. 2, pp. 85–93, doi.org/10.1111/j.1399-3038.2005.00366.x;

S Sausenthaler et al., 'Maternal diet during pregnancy in relation to eczema and allergic sensitization in the offspring at 2 y of age', *The American Journal of Clinical Nutrition*, 2007, vol. 85, no. 2, pp. 530–37, doi.org/10.1016/j.jaci.2008.10.049;

E von Mutius et al., 'Increasing prevalence of hay fever and atopy among children in Leipzig, East Germany', *The Lancet*, 1998, vol. 351, no. 9106, pp. 862–66, doi.org/10.1016/S0140-6736(05)78777-8

10. Polyunsaturated fats reduce cognitive ability

21. A Estrada, 'Hold the Mayo', *The Current*, 9 September 2014, www.news.ucsb.edu/2014/014386/hold-mayo;

W D Lassek & S J C Gaulin, 'Linoleic and docosahexaenoic acids in human milk have opposite relationships with cognitive test performance in a sample of 28 countries', *Prostaglandins, Leukotrienes & Essential Fatty Acids (PLEFA)*, November 2014, vol. 91, no. 5, pp. 195–201, doi.org/10.1016/j.plefa.2014.07.017;

W D Lassek & S J C Gaulin, 'Sex Differences in the Relationship of Dietary Fatty Acids to Cognitive Measures in American Children', *Frontiers in Evolutionary Neuroscience*, 2 November 2011, vol. 3, no. 5, doi.org/10.3389/fnevo.2011.00005;

E M Novak et al., 'High dietary omega-6 fatty acids contribute to reduced docosahexaenoic acid in the developing brain and inhibit secondary neurite growth', *Brain Research Journal*, 27 October 2008, vol. 1237, pp. 136–45, doi.org/10.1016/j.brainres.2008.07.107;

11. Polyunsaturated fats degrade a man's ability to have children

21. A Agarwal et al., 'Role of reactive oxygen species in the pathophysiology of human reproduction', *Fertility and Sterility*, April 2003, vol. 79, no. 4, pp. 829–843, doi.org/10.1016/S0015-0282(02)04948-8;

R J Aitken & C Krausz, 'Oxidative stress, DNA damage and the Y chromosome', *Reproduction*, October 2001, vol. 122, no. 4, pp. 497–506, doi.org/10.1530/reprod/122.4.497;

R J Aitken et al., 'Reactive Oxygen Species and Sperm Function – In Sickness and In Health', *Journal of Andrology*, vol. 33, no. 6, November–December 2012, pp. 1096–1106, doi.org/10.2164/jandrol.112.016535;

E Carlsen et al., 'Evidence for decreasing quality of semen during past 50 years', *BMJ*, 1992, vol. 305, pp. 609–13, www.ncbi.nlm.nih.gov/pmc/articles/PMC1883354/;

S H Swan et al., 'The question of declining sperm density revisited: an analysis of 101 studies published 1934–1996', *Environmental Health Perspectives*, 2000, vol. 108, no. 10, pp. 961–66, www.ncbi.nlm.nih.gov/pmc/articles/PMC1240129/;

A Lenzi et al., 'Lipids of the sperm plasma membrane: from polyunsaturated fatty acids considered as markers of sperm function to possible scavenger therapy', *Human Reproductive Update*, 1 May 1996, vol. 2, no. 3, pp. 246–56, doi.org/10.1093/humupd/2.3.246;

M R Safarinejad et al., 'Relationship of omega-3 and omega-6 fatty acids with semen characteristics, and anti-oxidant status of seminal plasma: A comparison between fertile and infertile men', *The American Journal of Clinical Nutrition*, 2010, vol. 29, no. 1, pp. 100–105, www.clinicalnutritionjournal.com/article/S0261-5614(09)00158-7/fulltext;

K Tremellen, 'Oxidative stress and male infertility – a clinical perspective', *Human Reproduction Update*, vol. 14, no. 3, May–June 2008, pp. 243–258, doi.org/10.1093/humupd/dmn004

L Yan et al., 'Effect of different dietary omega-3/omega-6 fatty acid ratios on reproduction in male rats', *Lipids in Health and Disease*, 13 March 2013, vol. 12, no. 33, doi.org/10.1186/1476-511X-12-33

And we don't even need to eat them to suffer

23. According to the Australian Institute . . .: Australian Institute of Health and Welfare (AIHW), 'Cancer in Australia 2017', Australian Government, 3 February 2017, www.aihw.gov.au/reports/cancer/cancer-in-australia-2017/related-material

In 2018, it was 379 people . . .: Cancer Australia, 'All cancers in Australia', Australian Government, 2019, canceraustralia.gov.au/affected-cancer/what-cancer/cancer-australia-statistics

2. Identifying polyunsaturated fats

If you're interested in what our diet looked like prior to industrialisation (in particular the ratio of the various fats), read: S B Eaton & M Konner, 'Paleolithic Nutrition: A consideration of its nature and current implications', *New England Journal of Medicine*, 1985, vol. 312, no. 5, pp. 283–9, doi.org/10.1056/NEJM198501313120505

Omega-3 and omega-6 fatty acids

27. What they do know is that . . .: T L Blasbalg et al., 'Changes in consumption of omega-3 and omega-6 fatty acids in the United States during the 20th century', *The American Journal of Clinical Nutrition*, 2011, vol. 93, no. 5, pp. 950–62, doi.org/10.3945/ajcn.110.006643

Baby formula

For information on breastfeeding rates in Australia, see: www.health.gov.au/internet/main/publishing.nsf/Content/health-pubhlth-strateg-brfeed-index.htm

Statistics on the world baby-food market can be found at: www.statista.com/statistics/719436/global-market-size-baby-formula/

72. Studies on various populations clearly . . .: A E Hansen et al., 'Essential fatty acid in infant nutrition. III. Clinical manifestations of linoleic acid deficiency', *The Journal of Nurition*, 10 December 1958, vol. 66, no. 4, 565–76.
73. Babies need omega-6 and omega-3 fats . . .: L Lauritzen et al., 'The essentiality of long chain n-3 fatty acids in relation to the development and function of the brain and retina' 2001, *Progress in Lipid Research*, 40: 1–94.

Bacon and pork

66. In reality, only about 5 per cent . . .: Agrifutures Australia, 'Pigs for Meat (Pork)', 24 May 2017, www.agrifutures.com.au/farm-diversity/pigs-meat-pork/
67. Most pig meat comes from animals farmed . . .: Annual Pork Limited, *Australian Industry Survey*, 2017, australianpork.com.au/wp-content/uploads/2018/07/Annual-Industry-Survey-2017-FINAL.pdf
     Only 4.7 per cent of Australian pigs . . .: Australian Pork Limited, *Australian Pig Annual*, 2012–13, auspigannual.realviewdigital.com/#folio=

Eggs and chicken

The Australian Government's Australian Guide to Healthy Eating (https://www.eatforhealth.gov.au/sites/default/files/content/The%20Guidelines/n55_agthe_large.pdf)

Two major egg trials are written up in 'A Prospective Study of Egg Consumption and Risk of Cardiovascular Disease in Men and Women', Journal of the American Medical Association, 1999; 281(15): 1387–1394 (DOI: 10.1001/jama.281.15.1387) and the 2006 review showing that egg consumption converts you to Pattern A is 'Dietary cholesterol provided by eggs and plasma lipoproteins in healthy populations', Current Opinion in Clinical Nutrition & Metabolic Care 9 (1): 8–12.

National Health and Medical Research Council 2017, *Eat for Health: Australian Dietary Guidelines Summary,* Department of Health and Ageing, 2013, www.eatforhealth.gov.au/sites/default/files/files/the_guidelines/n55a_australian_dietary_guidelines_summary_book.pdf;

Fernandez, 'Dietary cholesterol provided by eggs and plasma lipoproteins in healthy populations', *Current Opinion in Clinical Nutrition & Metabolic Care*, January 2006, vol. 9, no. 1, pp. 8–12, doi.org/10.1097/01.mco.0000171152.51034.bf;

F B Hu et al., 'A prospective study of egg consumption and risk of cardiovascular disease in men and women', *JAMA*, April 1999, vol. 281, no. 15, pp. 1387–1394, doi:10.1001/jama.281.15.1387

Acknowledgements

When I decided that our family would no longer eat sugar, my wife, Lizzie, put in the thousands of hours of trial and error needed to create sweet recipes from my chosen substitute, glucose. When I subsequently decided we were no longer to eat foods high in polyunsaturated fats, I really threw her a curve ball. We quickly discovered that very little food in our local supermarket satisfied a rule that excluded both fructose and seed oils. What fructose was to the (largely) dessert menu, seed oils were to everything else we ate.

Suddenly we could no longer buy most supermarket bread. Cracker biscuits were gone. Meat pies were history. Indeed, anything with pastry was probably off the menu. And forget Friday-night-off-for-the-cook fish and chips. But Lizzie stepped into the breach and got to work. Her aim was not just to assemble a recipe collection, but also to make sure the recipes were easy and fuss-free enough for a busy mum or dad to make on a daily basis. Bread that required two hours of kneading was not an option.

Once again, Lizzie has pulled it off. She has put together a terrific collection of really usable everyday recipes and I can't express my gratitude enough. Without her efforts, the practical part of this book would be very sadly lacking (well, actually, non-existent).

The taste-testing crew (otherwise known as our kids) of Anthony, James, Gwen, Adam, Elizabeth and Fin also deserve special commendation. They have come a long way in their sugar-free travels. It was a big deal to ask them to accept that very little processed food at all would be in their future. Before this book they were getting through a loaf of supermarket bread a day. Now they have none. And that is just one of the major changes our kids have had to take in their stride in the past year or so. They have done it with good humour and even (in some cases) down-right joy. Both Lizzie and I are very grateful for their participation in our stampede towards a DIY food supply (see how I made that sound like they had a choice).

I continue to be amazed at the generosity that is shown by our friends and family. Once again the brains in the kitchen at our local school, Tatjana and then, towards the end, Marianne, were a great inspiration with recipe ideas. Anyone who has our company foisted upon them can't help but be affected. I'm grateful to them all but once again, Beth, Melinda and Mandy stand out with their interest in (and, at times, assistance with) our olde worlde food experiments. The same goes for our family, in particular Beth and Tony (who listen a lot whether they want to or not) and Adam, Sarah, Laura and Wendy who spend their holidays as guinea pigs (with a level of tolerance that is truly impressive).

Nicole Long, Katrina O'Brien, Jocelyn Hungerford and the rest of the team at Penguin did a fabulous job of creating the first version of this book way back in 2013. The newly updated and improved version you now hold in your hands was remoulded by Ariane Durkin and Libby Turner at Pan Macmillan. At both Penguin and Pan Mac, Ingrid Ohlsson was once again the truly visionary publisher.

My good friend Frank Stranges as usual stood around and did nothing (and expects to be paid for it) – otherwise known as taking care of all the agency business-type stuff.

Index